Unconditional Love

BRIAN SMITH

PublishAmerica
Baltimore

First printing

ISBN: 1-4137-6066-X
PUBLISHED BY PUBLISHAMERICA, LLLP
www.publishamerica.com
Baltimore

Printed in the United States of America

DEDICATION

This book is dedicated to my father, Willis. Over the years we have had our ups and our downs. As I gradually emerged out of the chaotic time known as the teenage years, I can honestly say that he became much wiser as I became older. It wasn't that he wasn't already wiser in a lot of things; it was my growing to realize and appreciate what he already knew oftentimes. Throughout all the changes I have gone through, he has remained faithful in his relationship to me, even when I was not always faithful to him. He has not only been my daddy, but my friend, and I can truly say that in this, he has been a living example to me of the Father's commitment in love.

Thanks, Daddy, for not only sticking it out with me, but for validating me with your love, your friendship, and your trust.

Your son,
Brian

This book is intended as spiritual advice only, and is not intended to be considered as or in lieu of professional advice in any given matter. For such, please see a qualified or licensed advisor.

The identity and some of the circumstances of individuals cited apart from Bible text have been intentionally altered to protect and preserve the privacy of the individuals involved.

OTHER PUBLISHED BOOKS BY BRIAN SMITH

The Art of Waging Spiritual Warfare in the 21ˢᵗ Century

FORTHCOMING/UNPUBLISHED BOOKS

Love's Desire

The House That Wisdom Built

Once Saved Always Saved

Out of the Darkness and Into the Light

Are Demons & Fallen Angels One In the Same?

*Governing Your Passions & Controlling Your Lust
a.k.a. The Pride of Life & The Lust of the Flesh*

TABLE OF CONTENTS

PROLOGUE ❖ 13

CHAPTER ONE ❖ 15
The History

CHAPTER TWO ❖ 18
Marry a Woman of Whoredom

CHAPTER THREE ❖ 27
Flaming Hot Love—What's in a Name?

CHAPTER FOUR ❖ 41
Not Pitied—The Dilemma of Tough Love

CHAPTER FIVE ❖ 48
Not My People—The Bill of Estrangement

CHAPTER SIX ❖ 57
Violation and Atrocity

CHAPTER SEVEN ❖ 72
The Road to Restoration and Reconciliation

CHAPTER EIGHT ❖ 79
Fifteen Pieces of Silver

CHAPTER NINE ❖ 92
The Sins of the Fathers—The Indictment

CHAPTER TEN ❖ 105
Check Please—The Verdict

BIBLIOGRAPHY ❖ 113

Unconditional Love

PROLOGUE

Nestled between the books of Daniel and Joel, well within the heart of the Old Testament, lies the little book of Hosea. Not numerous in chapters as say, perhaps, the books of Genesis or Isaiah, but still very potent in its message, for you see, within its pages lie a message, a picture, a very candid and intimate portrait of God the Father's love for His people. Not a love as most men would reckon love, but a love that is pure—strong yet tender, though tough at times, still nevertheless, never afraid to lay itself upon the alter of sacrifice. In 1 Corinthians 13:1-3 the Apostle Paul said of this love:

> Though I speak with the tongues of men and of angels, and have not charity, I am become as sounding brass, or a tinkling cymbal.
>
> And though I have the gift of prophecy, and understand all mysteries, and all knowledge; and though I have all faith, so that I could remove mountains, and have not charity, I am nothing.
>
> And though I bestow all my goods to feed the poor, and though I give my body to be burned, and have not charity, it profiteth me nothing.

This small, yet potent book of Hosea reveals something that few people, I dare say even true believers, have yet to fathom—an eternal God who wants to, is willing to, and actively continues to convey His unconditional love to all people. Hosea is not just the story of a love gone wrong in the life of a man or a nation that had lost its way, but it is the portrait of the Father's love that cries: "How shall I give thee up!" (Hosea 11:8a). Its preeminent theme and challenge to the individual is covenant **fidelity**.

True love beareth all things, believeth all things, hopeth all things, endureth all things, and never fails (paraphrase—1 Corinthians 13:7-8a). Love is an action word, and God is a God of action. Hosea is the Gospel (Good News) pre-incarnate. Not only is Hosea a call to the nations from the Living Eternal God, but also it is a challenge to all believers to woo people to God, by being living sermons of God's love, especially within their families. Mahatma Gandhi has been quoted by an unknown source to say:

> If my people were to see the Jesus of the Bible, they would readily embrace Him (body, soul, and spirit); but it is when we meet people who proclaim to follow him, that we are left disheartened.

While the nation of Israel (Ephraim), like Hosea's wife, "hath hired [her] lovers (Hosea 8:9)" and was guilty of the vilest adultery, nevertheless God the Father demonstrates through his faithful minister Hosea, that even in the midst of adultery, uncertainty, and heartache, there is forgiveness, redemption, and restoration. He is the committed lover who demonstrates in both thoughts and deeds that which He Himself calls for from all believers—unconditional love.

CHAPTER ONE
The History

The year is approximately 755 B.C. and King Jeroboam II is the ruler of the Northern Kingdom of Israel (also known as Ephraim) where the prophet Hosea was a citizen. Some 150-200 years prior (approximately 930 B.C.) the nation of Israel had split into two parts just after the death of King Solomon. Due to King Solomon's continual and massive building projects, many people had been heavily taxed and conscripted to perform the required labor needed for these projects. At the king's death, Jeroboam, the man whom Solomon had entrusted to oversee the conscripted laborers (1 Kings 11:28), along with others, confronted the new king, Rehoboam—Solomon's son (1 Kings 11:43), and asked him to lighten the taxes and physical loads his father had placed upon the nation of Israel during his reign.

Instead of heeding the wise council of the elders who stood before his father, he took the advice of the young men who had grown up with him and increased the taxes and workload (1 Kings 12:3-15). This decision resulted in Jeroboam leading ten of the twelve tribes to revolt and secede from the nation of Israel to form what later became the Northern Kingdom. Only the house of David, the tribes of Judah and Benjamin, remained faithful to the throne of King Rehoboam.

After the secession of the ten tribes of Israel (which at that time were comprised of Reuben, Simeon, Gad, Asher, Levi, Issachar, Zebulun, Dan, Naphtali, and the half tribes of Ephraim and Manasseh), many people in the Northern Kingdom became homesick for the temple in Jerusalem. While the people of the Northern Kingdom had approximately three times the geographical territory, extremely fertile pastureland, plains rich in minerals and vegetation for commercial export, still Jerusalem, well within the borders of the Southern Kingdom, was home to Solomon's Temple, and many longed to worship God there. Fearing that the people would eventually gravitate back to the Southern Kingdom, Jeroboam I established two major temples for worship inside of the borders of the Northern Kingdom. Not only did he not choose men from the tribe of Levi to minister in these temples, but also he dared to break God's second commandment (Exodus 20) by establishing calf gods for the people to pray before. Thus began the moral decay of the Northern Kingdom.

Over the next century and a half, the Northern Kingdom and the Southern Kingdom of Israel fought many battles against each other. The spiritual climate in the Southern Kingdom, while similar in many ways to its northern counterpart, did not degrade nearly as fast. Outwardly, largely in part to its fertile lands and agricultural resources, the Northern Kingdom prospered economically. Inwardly, however, the nation's soul and spirit were in a precarious situation. The priesthood became extremely corrupt, idolatry became rampant among the people, and the rich became richer, while the poor only became more oppressed. By the time King Jeroboam II reached the throne in approximately 793 B.C. (some 130+ years after Jeroboam I), spiritually the priests were not adhering to the Levitical rights or laws given to them from God through Moses. **Many were living an idolatrous, hedonistic lifestyle in which they denied themselves no earthly pleasures.** The nation as a whole lacked moral leadership and had strayed from its upbringing.

Politically at the time, when Jeroboam II took over the reign of the Northern Kingdom, the nation's borders and security were extremely uncertain. Four of the past six kings had been assassinated. Egypt, still considered the predominant world power, along with the other nations of the world, began to see and feel the power of the Assyrian nation as it began to emerge as the dominating force on the world scene. Within one lifetime of King Jerobaom II's death, Israel, along with Egypt and other nations, would fall prey to the ravenous appetites and conquest of Assyrian greats such as Tigleth-Pilaser III. It is here, in the midst of uncertainty, political chaos, and rampant moral debauchery, that the Lord raised up a man after his own heart by the name of Hosea, the son of Beeri (Hosea 1:1).

CHAPTER TWO
Marry a Woman of Whoredom

The word of the LORD that came unto Hosea, the son of Beeri, in the days of Uzziah, Jotham, Ahaz, and Hezekiah, kings of Judah, and in the days of Jeroboam the son of Joash, king of Israel.

The beginning of the word of the LORD by Hosea. And the LORD said to Hosea, "Go, take unto thee a wife of whoredoms and children of whoredoms: for the land hath committed great whoredom, departing from the LORD" (Hosea 1:1-2).

When I was growing up in the sixties, one of the things I loved the most was Motown music: Martha Reeves & the Vandellas, The Temptations, Four Tops, and the Supremes. One of my favorite songs sang by the Supremes was "Ain't No Mountain High Enough." I especially liked the part of the chorus that went:

There ain't no mountain high enough
Ain't no valley low enough
Ain't no river wide enough
To keep me from getting to you

Remember the day
I set you free
I told you
You could always count on me
From that day on I made a vow
I'll be there...

While I understand some of you may take exception with this statement, these lyrics tend to express the heart of God in these opening verses of Hosea. Immediately in Hosea 1:1 The Self Existent One Who Reveals Himself (Jehovah or LORD in all capital letters) chooses a man by the name of Hosea to deliver His message of love, hope, and restoration to the nation of Israel. God could have easily chosen the prophets Isaiah, Micah, or Amos to deliver this particular message to Israel, for they too lived during the time of Hosea, but the Sovereign of all things elected to chose a preacher whose name meant "deliverer" or "salvation." When you really think about it, not only are the love of God and the heart of God displayed in these opening two verses, but also the entire message of the Gospel of Jesus Christ is intricately woven into the verses as well.

Remember in Deuteronomy 7:7-8 when pastor Moses was on God's holy mountain talking about the nation of Israel? God told him:

The LORD did not set his love upon you, nor choose you, because ye were more in number than any people; for ye were the fewest of all people:

But because the LORD loved you, and because he would keep the oath which he had sworn unto your fathers, hath the LORD brought you out with a mighty hand, and redeemed you.

Why did God choose Israel? Because **He loved her** (the nation) **first.** The heart of God is His people. When I was in bible college, one of my instructors told me that if one were to "come boldly unto the throne of grace" (Hebrews 4:16), crawl up into God's lap, and lay your head across God's heart, you would in all likelihood not hear God's heart go "thump..thump..thump," but "people..people..people." Contrary to what many would have you believe, **true love is not an emotion or feeling** that you have no control over. True love is and always has been **an act of each and every individual's divine and sovereign will**; therefore, the decision to love or not love someone is yours on a moment-by-moment continual basis. As it is with man's will, even more so is it with the will of God. **True love is a commitment.** I would even go so far as to say a lifelong covenant (of commitment and fidelity) when one is married, **that determines to seek the highest good of the other no matter what**.

In the New Testament, John 3:16 says: "God **so loved** the World, that he gave his only begotten Son, that whosoever believeth in him should not perish, but have everlasting life."

The phrase "so loved" actually carries with it the nuance of "having loved at first or beforehand." See, here it is again just as it was in Deuteronomy 7:7-8. "What is God, a God of love, who loves others, even when they are not necessarily faithful to Him!"

Once God had established his covenant (betrothal or engagement if you will) with Israel (Genesis 17:9), Israel, as the espoused (engaged) to God, broke its vows with Him. Jeremiah 3:20 says:

Surely as a wife treacherously departeth from her husband, so have ye dealt treacherously with me, O house of Israel, saith the LORD.

All *ye* like sheep have gone astray; *ye* have turned every one to his own way (Isaiah 53:6).

"But in the fullness of the time, God sent forth his Son, made of a woman, made under the law, to redeem them that were under the law, that we might receive the adoption of sons" (Galatians 4:4-5). This same God who required the anointed cherub Lucifer and other angels to come up to His Holy Mountain to worship Him (Ezekiel 28:14), crowned mankind with glory and honor (Genesis 1:26,Psalms 8:5), received unto Himself in covenant Abraham and his seed as an espoused (Genesis 17:9), brought Israel out of slavery in Egypt with a mighty hand (Exodus 13), only to have her (Israel) deal with Him **"as a wife treacherously departeth from her husband [...] for the land hath committed great whoredom, departing from the LORD."** Now in Hosea 1:2, with the utmost expression of love, God sends forth a living message (and messenger) of salvation (redemption) to His beloved, the prophet Hosea. This is the mystery and the revelation power of the Good News (Gospel). A God who by His very nature is perfect and holy, seeking after a woman of whoredom and children of whoredoms: "For the Son of man is come to seek and to save that which was lost" (Luke 19:10). "For the land hath committed great whoredom" (Hosea 1:2).

I must say that over the years the LORD has allowed me to, for reasons only He Himself knows, be deeply involved in the chaos and anarchy of others' lives. While I am constantly reminding my children that there are three types of business (mind your own, none of yours, and if it doesn't bother you, don't you bother it),

I seem to periodically, and at times without warning, be caught at the epicenter of certain people's crisis. In all fairness, however, I must admit that if I adhere closely to the leading of the Holy Spirit, I usually am amazed at the eventual conclusion. Such was the case about seven or eight years ago when I had an opportunity to minister to a young man named John regarding his impending nuptials with a young lady named Kathy.

Kathy was young, bright, and full of life. She was a young lady who was very stately, proper, and a very promising talent in the world of journalism. She was to the best of his knowledge a born-again believer and very charismatic, yet private when it came to her dealings with people. He could not have asked for a greater blessing in his life. Yet for all of Kathy's gifts and talents, there was still one thing that deeply disturbed John down within his soul—Kathy had several children, and they were all by different men! It was not that John did not deeply love Kathy, nor was it a matter of John not loving her children either, for without warning, John realized that not only had he unknowingly gravitated toward these children, but that he had also allowed the hearts of these children to be turned towards him. John wrestled deep within his soul as to whether or not he was up to the task of taking on children that were not his, dealing with non-custodial parents, and the stigma that people might associate with his newfound family if ever they found out that Kathy was not previously married and that all of her children had different biological fathers.

My response to John's personal crisis was for him to think about and consider his own personal salvation as it related to the revelation of the Gospel of Jesus Christ. His dilemma was no different than that of the prophet Hosea or even the Lord Jesus Christ. I explained to him that to fully understand and reconcile this stigma (marrying an individual who has children out of wedlock) being adding to his life, one only had to look at the motivation behind the revelation of the Gospel. Once you really and truly examine the Doctrine of Salvation and the covenant of marriage, you will find that they are actually inseparable at a foundational and fundamental level. The eternal security of every believer in Christ rests upon two things:

♦ God's ability to remain faithful to his Word, Covenants, and decisions.

♦ Jesus ability to sacrificially love mankind enough to lay down his life for all those who would believe upon him.

During his imprisonment in Rome, the Apostle Paul penned the Letter to the Ephesians, in which he admonished husbands to:

> ...love your wives, even as Christ also loved the church, and gave himself for it....So ought men to love their wives as their own bodies. He that loveth his wife loveth himself. For no man ever yet hated his own flesh; but nourisheth and cherisheth it, even as the Lord the church (Ephesians 5:26, 28-29).

This, too, is what 1 Corinthians Chapter 13 (The Love Chapter) is all about; *not just a love that looks good or* **makes you** *feel good*, but is committed no matter what. You see, if God can break his word to His espoused Israel (that I will in no ways cast you out), then why not His word regarding the salvation of believers? The marriage covenant is directly linked to the believer's eternal security, for they are both based on the same thing—the Eternal Love of God, which is an act of His Sovereign will. If, according to Scripture, mankind is made in the exact express image of God (Genesis 1:27), then what is true of God should also be true between a husband and wife, with regard to commitment and devotion.

Love is a decision and a commitment to seek another's utmost good, even at one's own expense. For the Son of man came to save (*redeem, make whole, and reunite*) that which was lost (Matthew 18:11). 2 Peter 3:9 says: "The Lord is not slack concerning his promise, as some men count slackness; but is longsuffering to us-ward, not willing that any should perish."

In Christ, God has a place for everyone. God does not make junk and God has no spare parts. Every life that is created is created by the One True Sovereign Lord with meaning, definite purpose within His will, and out of His love. Jesus said: "Suffer little children, and forbid them not, to come unto me: for of such is the kingdom of heaven" (Matthew 19:14).

Therefore, not only does God not want anyone lost, He highly values children as well. They are not second-class citizens or chattel (property). Upon all of this is the entire purpose and mystery of the Gospel, the Plan (doctrine) of Salvation, and covenant of marriage. A world full of people estranged from God and rocketing down the express lane to hell is redeemed (saved, delivered, rescued, made whole) by a loving God who looked beyond their faults and saw the needs. "All we like sheep had gone astray; we had turned every one to his own way" (Isaiah 53:6), but the **Son of man came to save that which was lost**.

I explained to John that Proverbs 18:22 says that "**Whosoever findeth a wife findeth a good thing, and obtaineth favour of the LORD**." If he married Kathy, she would become by God's own declaration his (John's) "good thing," and that God was extending to him an opportunity to obtain additional favor of the LORD. God was giving him an opportunity to model (live out), before others, the underlying covenants of the same salvation through which Jesus had made him (John) a citizen of Heaven. Who cares what people think about Kathy's past? When Jesus walked the earth, people talked about him! In John 8:1-3, the scribes and Pharisees brought a woman to Jesus taken in adultery. They had caught her physically in the act and brought her to Jesus to be condemned and in all likelihood be put to death, but by the time you reach verses 10-11, Jesus says:

> "Woman, where are those thine accusers? Hath no man condemned thee?" She said, "No man, Lord." And Jesus said unto her, "**Neither do I condemn thee: go, and sin no more.**"

I said to John, "Jesus does not condemn Kathy, so who is anyone else—including you—to condemn her or go digging around in her past? Realize that Jesus has, according to Isaiah 1;18, said 'Come now [Kathy], and let us reason together, saith the LORD: though your sins be as **scarlet,** they shall be as white as snow; though they be red like crimson, they shall be as wool.' Kathy has repented, turned her life around by the grace and mercy of Jesus Christ, been washed in the forgiving blood of Jesus, and now God is presenting her to you as your 'good thing,' with favor. The question now is whether you are man enough to trust that God has your best interest at heart—unconditional love—in presenting Kathy to you as a bride.

"With regard to Kathy's children, remember that children are:

♦ An heritage [heirloom, inheritance, a portion] of the LORD (Psalms 127:3).

♦ Children's children are the crown of old men (Proverbs 17:6).

"In the Old Testament, one of the indicators people used to measure a man's prosperity and the favor of God upon his life was by the number of children that he had, and indeed grandchildren. If children are an inheritance or heirloom according to Psalms 127:3, then in taking on the challenges and responsibilities of Kathy's children, you are also gaining another man's inheritance. Evidently, for whatever His reasons, God thinks highly of you enough that he is willing to entrust you with the awesome privilege of raising another man's children. He is willing to bestow upon you the honor of leading them back to Him, and in the process giving you the blessings that others would have been given in raising these particular children. God is not offering you hand-me-downs or second-hand goods, but has called in a specialist to get the job done on his behalf. You're God's preferred specialist or Top Gun if you want to be. It is not the children's fault that they are here, and if they are here, evidently God has a divine purpose for their lives, and is also giving you an opportunity to be a part of their part in Jesus ministry also."

Here again, the questions or issues were not as much about Kathy or her children, as they were about the opportunities from God to John for walking out the same grace, mercy, and salvation that all believers in Christ have.

In case you were wondering what the ultimate outcome of the conversation between John and myself was: He, Kathy, and their children were united in marriage the following spring.

CHAPTER THREE

Flaming Hot Love— What's in a Name?

Ask any of my children and they will quickly attest to the fact that I am an avid fan of old movies, especially the classics: *Maltese Falcon, Sweet Georgia Brown, The Wizard of Oz,* et cetera. As I began this chapter, my mind wondered over to and came to rest upon a scene from the movie classic *A Fiddler on the Roof.* During one particular scene, Teviar (the main character) is wrestling with some personal issues, in particular the desires of his daughter to marry a man that he would not have selected for her. After some considerable talking to himself, he looks up toward the beamingly bright skies of Heaven and says: "Lord, I know that we are the chosen people; but once in a while, could you pick somebody else..."

There are times in every individual's life, whether man or woman, adult or child, wealthy or poor, born-again or not, that they ask the rhetorically cynical question "Why me, Lord?" or

"Lord, so what did I do to deserve such an honor?" Although the expression may be somewhat sarcastic, the desire to know or understand why God allows certain individuals to partake of certain assignments still rings true. These are just some of the questions that Hosea is wrestling with internally as he goes forward to carry out the will of the Lord. At the heart of the question "Why me, Lord?" is not God calling Hosea to proclaim a message of love and redemption to a wayward nation, but the divine connection that must be consummated between Hosea and Gomer (the woman of whoredom).

Have you ever been out in public or been privileged to observe the union of two individuals that just seem to be so totally polarized or diverse in personality that you shake your head in awe and wonder: "How did those two people ever get together?" It's not that either party is necessarily unappealing to the eye; it's just that their backgrounds, interest, or personas would seem to clash like two cymbals in some quite study hall. Yet, for many, it is this bringing together of opposites or juxtaposing positions at just the right times that allows balance, harmony, or a sound worthy of a symphony to resonate throughout their lives.

I believe that, in everyone's life, God has appointed divine connections and divine appointments. **Divine appointments** are people or situations that you encounter, perhaps only once or else for a limited season of time in your life, but out of that encounter you receive epiphanies, insights, and such an infusion that it propels you into the next level of your life like a bullet fired from a high-powered rifle, as well as sets into place things that are with you for a lifetime. **Divine connections**, on the other hand, are people that you are destined to be associated with for life. There are certain things in life that you were literally born to do and certain people in life that you were born to reach or connect with, and only you can reach them or achieve this goal. If you do not do it, if you miss the opportunity, or you are not together with this particular individual, it or they could be permanently lost. The little mischievous boy in Sunday school might, with your help, grow up to be the next Billy Graham. That little girl whom you saved from drowning might be the one who grows up to find a cure for the terminal disease that your loved one will contract. Only Jesus, the Son of The Living God, could have redeemed a world that was lost, and without a doubt, you may literally be the only one standing between life and death, success or failure, in certain people's lives. You may be the only source of love and affection that some people will ever know.

Who else but the loving, gentle, tender, forgiving, and compassionate God, whose will it is that none "should perish, but that all should come to repentance" (2 Peter 3:9b), would place enough love and compassion in the heart of a preacher to allow him to marry a woman who was by profession a cult prostitute! Yes, you read this correctly—no exaggeration! This is the literal and loose translation of the phrase "wife of whoredom."

Cult prostitutes (including men or sodomites), who were called "men" or "women of whoredom," were the people who practiced or participated in religions that believed the fertility of their crops and prosperity of their herds were governed by the sexual relations (intercourse) between their gods. Therefore, sexual intercourse with the cult priests, priestesses, or cult prostitutes was an act of worship intended to mimic these gods and share in their powers of magic, reproduction, and fertility (1 Kings 14:21-24, 18:17-40).

This is the type of woman that the prophet Hosea was divinely called and appointed to pledge himself to in marriage. This was the woman that only he could minister to. This is the individual that he was destined to have as a lifelong connection. She was not necessarily a woman of high social esteem by most people's standards, but one who needed to receive salvation and loving grace from God nevertheless. Doesn't this sound just like what Jesus, the True Deliverer would do? Intimacy with tax collectors, harlots, and every other type of sinner.

For those of you who have been in or are in a life of prostitution, homosexuality, lesbianism, transvestitism, transsexuality, or even devil worshiping, God loves you and wants to reconcile you to Himself (Hosea 1:2). It is the lifestyle or actions of your life that God has a problem with, not you! There is no one who is so bad that God is not willing to save them right now.

SELAH

This is Hebrew for stop and really mediate on this one for a while—see Psalms 3:2,4 for an example.

And so it was, that in the season that the LORD commanded, Hosea, the minister and faithful servant of God, went to marry, "Gomer the daughter of Diblaim; which conceived, and bare him a son" (Hosea 1:3).

Someone once made the statement, "What's in a name?" Well, a lot if your name is Gomer! Imagine, if you will, the LORD God Almighty coming to you, the man or woman of God who is of Jewish descent (yes, there are awesome men and women of God who sold out to Jesus as Savior, and were born Jewish) telling you that He wants to use your life to demonstrate His unconditional love and ministry to His espoused Israel. That would certainly be no problem for many, and if you are really familiar with Scripture you might shout Isaiah 58:9 to the LORD by saying, "Here I am, send me LORD." The LORD, in response to your statement of availability, then asks you the same thing that Jesus asked his disciple Peter three times: "Lovest thou me more than these?" (John 21:15).

You, being eager to serve Jesus like Peter, respond: "Yea, Lord; thou knowest that I love thee" (John 21:15). So the LORD tells you that He wants you to go against all that you have been raised to believe and honor by marrying a non-Jew, and a person who is a known cult prostitute, only to immediately start having and raising children together.

At this point most people would be in the same situation as the Apostle Peter in Acts 11:5-10, where the Lord told him to slay and eat a host of animals that were considered to be unholy, unclean, and forbidden foods. After the initial shock and a loving rebuke by the Lord, "What God hath cleansed, that call not thou common [meaning beneath you or polluted]" (Acts 11:15b), you submit to the Heart of the LORD, and you, like the Apostle Peter had to, realize that the LORD is no respecter of persons, for "all people are equal in His eyesight" (Acts 11:16-18).

So you go and search for the spouse that the LORD would lead you to, and you discover that this person's name is Gomer. Incidentally, the name Gomer means "burning coals" or "enough," as in judgment or a situation that is a more than you can handle. Gomer's name then causes you to remember Proverbs 6:27-28 which says: "Can a man take fire in his bosom, and his clothes not be burned? Can one go upon hot coals, and his feet not be burned?"

Yes, Gomer was definitely not going to be the calm, easygoing type of woman. It is now at this point that you begin to see God's plan revealed on a larger scale and realize the magnitude of what the LORD has called you to do. The LORD is calling you to exchange the righteousness that you have in Him with that of this person named Gomer. To share your life and all that you are with one who most people would consider unredeemable, not worthy of real love, unworthy of "your greatness," and one who would be considered by society to be from the lowest grade of people socioeconomically, for her father's name ("Diblaim") literally meant "two fig cakes." People who could not afford to give much for the price of a dowry (a marriage present that ensured the new wife's financial security against the possibility her husband might forsake her or might die) usually gave fig cakes. Fig cakes were also part of most pagan ritual offerings.

Overwhelming though it may be for the prophet Hosea or anyone who would find themselves in this type of situation, this union of opposites is further enhanced by the birth of their first child Jezreel. For those of you who do not know, per custom and law for the ancient nation of Israel, children born of a harlot were not considered full heirs, but bastardized (inferior, not genuine, illegitimate, impure) progeny that were only marginally to be recognized at best (Genesis 38:24). Sounds strange, sure, but this is the ministry to which Hosea, and perhaps even you, are called by the LORD. This is how you might have to exhibit the heart of God. Remember that love is a commitment and marriage a lifelong commitment that does not cease just because you don't feel like living up to your part of the covenant that day.

So what happens when the righteousness of the LORD, as ministered through one whose name literally means "deliverer" (Hosea), is joined in legal binding covenant (marriage) to one whose name means "burning coals" (Gomer), as in judgment? The result is the unconditional love of God, and the mystery of the Gospel revealed. When Jesus came to the cross, "all our righteousness was as filthy rags" (Isaiah 64:6), yet He exchanged His righteousness for all believers' unrighteousness. Because of His true love, now all believers are the righteousness of God (2 Corinthians 5:21) and joint heirs with Christ (Romans 8:17). This type of selfless act on behalf of Jesus is true love in action, and the commitment to which all believers, including Hosea, obligated themselves at the time of their deliverance.

So the prophet Hosea, having taken Gomer, the daughter of Diblaim, to be bone of his bones, and flesh of his flesh (Genesis 2:23), gave his heart and love to Gomer his wife, so that she conceived and bore Hosea a son—a male heir to his lineage.

And the LORD said unto him, Call his name Jezreel [God sows or scatters]; for yet a little while, and I will avenge the blood of Jezreel upon the house of Jehu, and will cause to cease the kingdom of the house of Israel. And it shall come to pass at that day, that I will break the bow of Israel in the valley of Jezreel.

This passage in Hosea 1:4-5 illustrates a very important key to maintaining a love that flourishes, and that is to allow God into every aspect of your lives. The LORD is so committed to His espoused, and the believer in Christ, that He desires to be involved in every decision, every facet of their life. Husbands and wives should be this way with each other as well. Not in a domineering, dictatorial, or suffocating manner, but in a manner which illustrates to their mate that they are supportive of the challenges and opportunities that are presented before them. This not only promotes intimacy when you are involved in the decisions regarding each other's lives, but it promotes active and open dialogue, which staves off attacks in your relationship via innuendo, suspicion, or misrepresentation. This dialogue between God, spouse, and yourself is that three-fold cord that is not quickly broken that wise old King Solomon spoke about (Ecclesiastes 4:12). This is part of the reason that the LORD takes the initiative in naming the children of Hosea and Gomer. There is no decision too small or great that the LORD does not want to be at the center of in your life. Communication is such a vital key to maintaining a healthy relationship, and even the names of an individual convey messages to your peers.

To this day I am continually astonished at the destiny, the blessings, and curses parents unwittingly pronounce on their children when they decide on a name for their child. I once knew of a woman whose name was Josephine (which means seductress or temptress), and she, from all indications, lived up to this reputation. 1 Samuel 25:25 mentions a man whose name was Nabal (being interpreted to mean fool, stupid, or idiot) and he acted accordingly. Life and death are in the power of the tongue (Proverbs 18:21). Sociologists, psychologists, and pediatricians all agree that children often grow up to become whatever it is that their parents or important adult figures call, preach, or accuse them of being. "You'll never amount to anything." "Why do you have to be so stupid?" "Can't you do anything right?" "Look at Nana's little jailbird," or some other seemingly innocent witticism. Yet within a matter of a decade or so, the family is in crisis, going through counseling, and Nana's little cutie is on death row or serving a life sentence. Why? Simply put, it's the power of your words. As a man thinks (whatever people hear from loved ones regularly, whatever internal images they create for themselves) so he is (or tends to become).

I have one daughter who over the years I have affectionately referred to as Runt, because she was born premature. She has been a constant source of pride and joy to me over the years, but it wasn't until several years ago that I actually took notice of the fact that, although a middle child, Runt was only about two inches taller than her sisters, who were at least five years younger. Then it occurred to me what I had inadvertently decreed upon my daughter. I had for years, in calling her Runt, foretold smallness of stature. So these days we call her something else, which means taller. I'll admit that this may seem rather superstitious, but consider the fact that God spoke over Creation in Genesis 1 and it became so. Abraham, Isaac, and Jacob pronounced curses and blessings upon their children and to quote Genesis 1:7: "it was so."

So what's in a name? Only the shaping of your child's destiny! This is one of the reasons it is so vital to consider what you name or say to your children. This is part of the reason God Himself instructs Hosea to give his first-born child the name Jezreel. God is attempting to shape not only the destiny of a child, but set into place the future of an entire nation, and in order to facilitate that future for the nation of Israel, God has to do something that I find, even for myself after more than fourteen years of marital experience, extremely challenging, and that is dealing with root causes or unresolved issues.

I do not think that families or couples, especially in Western cultures, fully comprehend just how quickly and to what extent they create havoc in relationships by attacking loved ones with their words, especially in areas in which the other individual is already insecure, or by leaving any issue unresolved. Unresolved issues tend to do the most harm to an individual's personal worth because they act like a cancerous tumor next to a vital organ. They may fester for days, weeks, and even years before bursting to the surface. This is often the situation when you hear about relatively quiet individuals suddenly erupting into cataclysmic, and on rare occasions, fatal behavior. Unresolved issues not only do not facilitate the three-fold cord connection that is necessary to maintain a healthy relationship, but often, over the course of years, lead to the desire of one or both parties to euphemize (mercy kill) the relationship, if not the other individual as well. Not willing that any should perish, especially His beloved Israel, God personally takes the initiative (Jezreel: God sows) in not only bringing up, but also providing a solution to Israel's unsettled past offense regarding the house of Jehu and the blood spilled in the valley of Jezreel.

Jehu, for you scholars of history, was a commander in charge of the king's army (2 Kings 9:1-10) who embarked on a violently bloody campaign that led him ultimately to the throne of Israel. During the process he murdered:

- ◆ Joram, the current king of Israel (2 Kings 9:21-26)
- ◆ Ahaziah, king of Judah (2 Kings 9:27-29)
- ◆ Jezebel, the queen of the former king Ahab, whom he had thrown out a high window so that her body splashed blood up against the palace walls and the ground below, and as prophesied, the dogs ate her carcass to the point where not much of her remained (2 Kings 9:30 -37)
- ◆ He had the seventy sons of King Ahab decapitated and their heads set in two piles at the entrance of the city (2 Kings 10:1)
- ◆ 42 of the brethren of King Ahaziah were slaughtered mercilessly as they journeyed to visit the king (Ahaziah) and his relatives (2 Kings 10:14-15)
- ◆ All the remaining relatives of King Ahab in Samaria were exterminated at his command (2 Kings 10:17)
- ◆ Every priest, priestess, and worshipper of Baal was slain during a solemn feast he had maliciously proclaimed for Baal (2 Kings 10:19-25)

It was not the taking of the lives of King Joram or the prophets of Baal that caused issues with the LORD, but the taking of the innocent blood of King Ahab's seventy children and all those associated with his house that was at issue (2 Kings 10:1-11).

Deuteronomy 19:10,13, and 1 Kings 2:31-34 make it perfectly clear that a curse or offense is charged against those who take innocent blood. Not only do they pay for this travesty of justice, but the people of the land suffer as well because they are harboring these criminals. I know it may seem kind of mean to some people, but God was very clear about these matters when He gave the Law to the Israelites in the desert after the Exodus. And even though Jehu may have had the best intentions, as do many couples or individuals, even the LORD has His limits when it comes to what may or may not be done by or to people in covenant relationships.

The Self Existent One Who Reveals Himself (LORD) isn't trying to be mean or vindictive in bringing up the past, for when resolved properly He forever forgets it (Isaiah 43:25, Psalms 103:12), but He does this so that He and his espoused Israel may heal and go on together in intimate communion.

> Your marriage to anyone is a lie and disaster is waiting to happen until you reach the point where you, your spouse, and the Lord can openly discuss, forgive, and forget an offense! **If you ever bring it up, then you haven't truly forgiven and forgotten.**

SELAH

As for Jehu, while his zeal or passion was honorable, great, and even refreshing, it is was not justification for his unwarranted behavior in the taking or destroying of innocent blood. Passion or zeal, when not fully submitted to the restraints and control of the LORD, is hurtful, to say the least, and usually ends up disastrous for all parties concerned even after just a short period of time.

This is why I, in my own marriage and in counseling others, warn about being overtly zealous, jealous, or the avenger of past offenses.

When married couples offend each other or believers grieve the Holy Ghost, they in essence sin or draw innocent blood, much in the same way that Jehu did. Not only is it an offense or violation against another, but they actually sin against their own body as well, for in Christ all believers, whether married or not, are of one body (1 Corinthians 6:18b, Proverbs 8:36, Ephesians 5:23), of which Christ is the head. If one part of The Body malfunctions (whether it be believer, husband, wife, child, ministry, company, et cetera) then the whole body (relationship) suffers.

> For the body is not one member, but many. If the foot shall say, Because I am not the hand, I am not of the body; is it therefore not of the body? And if the ear shall say, Because I am not the eye, I am not of the body; is it therefore not of the body....
>
> And whether one member suffer, all the members suffer with it; or one member be honoured, all the members rejoice with it. Now ye are the body of Christ, and members in particular. (1 Corinthians 12:14-16, 26-27)

For anyone, especially married couples, who thinks that their past can't ever affect their future, it is my sad duty to inform them that it most certainly can and usually does. You just can't disregard unresolved or past issues, nor cover them up and hope that they will die off somewhere. Whenever there are past offensives in any relationship that haven't been fully dealt with, wounds never heal properly; they inevitably set up an infection, become cancerous, and the relationship dies. This is usually what happens when couples cite "irreconcilable differences" or say "we just grew apart" as their reasons for getting a divorce. No, it is not! Nothing could be further from the truth! The fact of the matter is one or both people stop investing in the relationship. They stopped communicating and dealing with offenses; thus, the relationship withered. So while Israel may have stopped investing in their relationship with the LORD, He however did not stop investing in them or *YOU*. The LORD, like the gentleman and lover that He is, not only brings up the past unresolved issue, but offers a solution to the present problems in their relationship:

> "I will avenge the blood of Jezreel upon the house of Jehu, and will cause to cease the kingdom of the house of Israel. And it shall come to pass at that day, that I will break the bow of Israel in the valley of Jezreel."

The LORD is going to avenge the innocent blood that was shed in Jezreel by removing the present and future dynasty (house) of Jehu from power in Israel. His method: "break the bow of Israel in the valley of Jezreel." Israel, under the leadership of the house of Jehu, shall shortly suffer a crushing military defeat. Here again, the name Jezreel—"God sows or scatters"—is appropriate.

Sometimes in marriage, "I'm sorry" is not enough to fix things. In order to deal with past offenses sufficiently, some things have to be castrated or made impotent (symbol of a broken bow) before the healing can start, and the relationship continues. Old habits have to be broken, inappropriate behavior purged, restitution (both tangible and intangible) made. In the case of the LORD's relationship with His espoused Israel, money won't fix it, and buying things doesn't always fix things in the covenant relationship of marriage either. Love is an action word, and the offering of material goods without the actions of love behind it is meaningless!

If, however, there is appropriate corresponding action, coupled with patience and time, then in the case of a covenant relationship (unconditional love), there is a definite promise of a future ahead. Your past determines your present, and your present determines your future. So always deal with offenses or mistakes as quickly as possible no matter how painful. "**But if ye will not do so, behold, ye have sinned against the LORD: and be sure your sin will find you out**" (Numbers 32:23).

CHAPTER FOUR
Not Pitied—
The Dilemma of Tough Love

And she [Gomer] conceived again, and bare a daughter. And God said unto him, Call her name Loruhamah [meaning "not pitied or "no mercy"]: for I will no more have mercy upon the house of Israel; but I will utterly take them away.

But I will have mercy upon the house of Judah, and will save them by the LORD their God, and will not save them by bow, nor by sword, nor by battle, by horses, nor by horsemen (Hosea 1:6-7).

Verse six touches upon an issue that I am sorry to say is becoming a lost art in many homes, especially between married couples, and that is the dispensing of "tough love." Tough love does not involve domestic violence! Tough love is when someone dares to confront someone else, be it their spouse, child, relative, or the "friend that sticketh closer than a brother" (Proverbs 18:24), with all possible love, and humbly let him or her know that what he or she is doing is totally unacceptable. Tough love not only confronts the unacceptable behavior in the individual from a biblical perspective, but it is also loving enough if need be to "let go and let God," meaning leave the person totally on their own so that God may deal with them directly. For some, this may mean a temporary separation, with no offer of support. For others, it may mean that you have to turn your wayward child over to the authorities. For some, it may mean that you have to leave for a season—your home, associates, and all that is familiar or certain for that which is uncertain. But, even in the administration of tough love, *the goal is always—and forever should be—separation for the purposes of reconciliation.* Know that despite how much it may hurt, how long you have to endure the burden, and the hurdles that you may have to overcome or circumvent, you are:

- ♦ Loved (2 Thessalonians 2:16)
- ♦ Able to "do [endure] all things through Christ which strengtheth you" (Philippians 4:13)
- ♦ "Made the righteousness of God in him" (*Jesus*—2 Corinthians 5:21)
- ♦ Always protected "for he shall give his angels charge over thee" (Psalms 91:11)
- ♦ Never alone "for he hath said, I will never leave thee, nor forsake thee" (Hebrews 13:5b)

Jesus himself had hurdles and circumstances to overcome. He was charged with being the recipient of our tough love on behalf of the Father in order that all might be saved (reconciled) unto God.

Looking unto Jesus the author and finisher of our faith;
who for the joy that was set before him [that joy being
reconciliation of mankind with God] endured the cross,
despising the shame, and is set down at the right hand of
the throne of God (Hebrews 12:2).

The WORD (Jesus, who is God Almighty) became flesh and
was born of a virgin named Mary (John 1:14, Matthew 1:16).
Lived as a man doing good unto all that He came in contact with
(John 10:30-32), only to be brutally and "without mercy or pity"
(Loruhamah) murdered, crucified unto death for our personal
sins, even the sins of the very ones who were the mortal agents of
his earthly death. "He, who knew no sin, was made sin for us all"
(2 Corinthians 5:21). This crucifying of the Holy One (Jesus)
caused him to be temporarily separated from Father God
(because GOD will not be associated with sin), and so Jesus cried
out from the cross: "*Eli, Eli, lama sabachthani?* That is to say, My
God, my God, why hast thou forsaken me?" (Matthew 22:46,
Mark 15:34, Psalms 22:1).

What was the end result of this separation? Reconciliation!

And, behold, the veil of the temple was rent in twain
from the top to the bottom; and the earth did quake, and
the rocks rent; And the graves were opened; and many
bodies of the saints which slept arose, And came out of
the graves after his resurrection, and went into the holy
city, and appeared unto many (Matthew 27:51–53).

The Eternal Sovereign of the Universe, God Almighty,
stepped down from *His throne* in the heights of Glory, and with
His own hands ripped in two the veil in the Holy of Holies from
the very top to the bottom, signifying that no longer would God

have to separate Himself from man. No longer would a veil, priest, prophet, Satan, or any demon bound for hell, be able to keep mankind from fellowshipping with He who is Eternal. Now God could approach mankind, and mankind could "come boldly unto the throne of grace [directly], that we may obtain mercy, and find grace to help in time of need." Man was reconciled—able to fellowship with God again through acceptance of Jesus as Saviour (John 14:16), and Jesus himself was raised from the dead to now be seated at the right hand of God (Mark 16:19, Romans 8:34). So, you see, **God believes in tough love and temporary separations**, even if it means that sometimes it has to be administered without pity or mercy (*Loruhamah*), **but always with the end result being reconciliation**.

I have in my life been the recipient of and have been challenged by the Lord to deal with or administer tough love. I, for some reason, have always thought it was easier to experience personally tough love, than to administer it to others. I remember the day I was forced to deal with my mother on a deeply rooted issue utilizing tough love, and to this day, I think it was by far one of the most trying times for me.

My mother, who has been home with the Lord for more than a decade, was born with a genetic predisposition to alcohol. In short, because there were several generations of drinkers in her family, she was born susceptible to alcoholism; a vulnerability that I, by the grace of God, have never had to deal with and managed to avoid. In her late thirties or early forties, my mother, due to a host of reasons that aren't germane, began to drink more. At first gradually, then as situations and times became more demanding, the quantities of alcohol that she consumed grew. Although she was a closet drinker and none of us ever saw her so inebriated that she was falling down, lost control of her bladder, or passed out, it became apparent that there was a serious problem.

After many years of politely suggesting that she seek help, I had to do that which I found gut wrenching and to this day one of the most painful things I have ever had to do. I confronted my mother utilizing tough love. My mother had come over to our home and was scheduled to take our children out for the day to the zoo, a movie, and dinner. When she arrived, I could tell that she had had one or two drinks and I told her that I could not place my children at risk by allowing them to be around her until she had proven to me that she had sought help for her drinking problem. I further explained that she could possibly lose one of the children due to momentary confusion or become involved in a serious car accident. She was establishing precedents or values in their lives regarding drinking that I did not believe would ultimately lead to the best for them. Therefore, as the father of her grandchildren, whom she loved dearly, it was my obligation to protect them and her from the consequences that could precipitate from her drinking and driving.

At first she was dumbfounded and after about thirty seconds of silence she became extremely abusive and aggressive in her behavior. I explained that this didn't mean that her grandchildren wouldn't call her or that she was restricted from calling them, but that a period of separation was needed until such time as she could deal with this particular challenge in her life.

Here I was, still a young man who was forever going to his mother for counsel and wisdom on child raising, how to be the right kind of husband, and positive suggestions, challenging a woman who I knew at the core of my being could have, and at times did, put the fear of Almighty God in me mentally and physically. It pained me to see her leave that day with tears in her eyes. I felt as if I had violated some type of sacred trust or spiritual law and should be damned to hell for it. My guts (literally stomach) were in an upheaval for days, as I did not hear from my mother, nor did she return any of my phone calls.

My father wanted to know what I had done to so upset my mother, and dealing with him in those days was no joke. In my life, even though I had been emancipated (actually told it was time for me to leave by my father) from home for quite some time, when my daddy spoke, it was though Pharaoh himself was speaking to the Hebrews in slavery. Daddy was a force to be reckoned with and not easily denied. You just didn't ignore my father or anger him by messing with my mother. What had I done? I had done what I believed according to Scripture was the appropriate thing. I confronted a brother or sister in the Lord who had fallen—in love and humility, but it did not make things any easier.

A couple of weeks went by with no answer from my mother, and then it came. One of my younger sisters called and left me a message saying that our mother was in the hospital. I don't know why, but all the way to the hospital, I thought I would find her gone home to be with the Lord, and I would have allowed her to slip into eternity with our relationship on a bad note. Much to my relief, when I arrived at the hospital, I found my mother had checked herself into a substance abuse detoxification program and that she needed a family member to go through counseling with her. While anyone, including my father, could have done this with her, I think this was the Lord promoting healing in our relationship, her attempt to show me that she really was trying to make everything right between us, and perhaps to an even smaller extent, her revenge on me for making her cry.

I am happy to say that although my mother had some challenges and opportunities in remaining sober, the question of her being able to spend time with her grandchildren alone was never again an issue—even up until the day she went to be with Jesus.

Tough love is never easy for the recipient, nor is it an easy task for the one called upon to administer it. If you ever find yourself in a situation that requires tough love, or you are the one who is to confront another's behavior, never attack the individual personally, but always remain focused on the behavior. Please heed the wisdom of 1 John 5:16, Proverbs 3:6, and Galatians 6:1: Pray for them first.

> If any man see his brother sin a sin which is not unto death, he shall ask [pray], and he shall give him life for them that sin not unto death. There is a sin unto death: I do not say that he shall pray for it (1 John 5:16).

Secondly, let the Lord lead you as to the proper timing to confront the individual about the unacceptable behavior. Trust Him, and you will know exactly when the time is right to confront the behavior of the individual. "In all thy ways acknowledge him, and he shall direct thy paths" (Proverbs 3:6).

Finally, at the leading of the Holy Spirit of God, talk with that individual in a spirit of true humility, love, and gentleness, lest you be tempted and caught in doing the same thing. "Brothers, if someone is caught in a sin, you who are spiritual should restore him gently. But watch yourself, or you also may be tempted" (Galatians 6:1 – NIV).

Tough love is never easy, but to a repentant heart it is a wellspring of life.

SELAH

CHAPTER FIVE
Not My People—
The Bill of Estrangement

⁸Now when she had weaned Loruhamah, she conceived, and bare a son.

⁹Then said God, Call his name Loammi: for ye are not my people, and I will not be your God.

¹⁰Yet the number of the children of Israel shall be as the sand of the sea, which cannot be measured nor numbered; and it shall come to pass, that in the place where it was said unto them, Ye are not my people, there it shall be said unto them, Ye are the sons of the living God.

¹¹Then shall the children of Judah and the children of Israel be gathered together, and appoint themselves one head, and they shall come up out of the land: for great shall be the day of Jezreel.

I can't tell you how many times in my life I have witnessed to my utter most sorrow the manifestation of what the Lord is talking about here in Hosea 1:9. The hardest thing that I have ever had to bare witness to or endure was the whole idea of being "estranged." According to Webster's Encyclopedic Dictionary of the English Language, the word "estrangement" means: "to keep apart or out of friendly relations; to make to cease from being familiar; to alienate; or to turn from kindness to indifference."

Contrary to what the world might have one think, being estranged from someone does not mean that you are necessarily separated physically from another, nor does it imply that one is divorced or in the process of getting one. It simply means that two people are no longer on one accord **in a covenant relationship,** be it marital, business, family, or otherwise. Parents have children, yet don't know their likes or dislikes, who their friends are or what they do when they are not around them. Business partners go into the office every day, yet one can't stand the sight of the other, and the employees have divided loyalties. In a situation where two people are legally married, it is quite possible to live in the same house, raise children together, be physically intimate with each other, eat together every day for fifty years, and yet be estranged. She has his name and spends his money, while he uses her body and has her service his needs. Sad to say, many have lived this way, myself included. But praise God that this is no longer the situation in my own personal life.

Too many couples or families are comfortable with each other's presence in their lives, but very well could have never taken the time to get to really know each other nor be involved in each other's lives; therefore, they grow indifferent, cold, and finally callous toward one another. This callousness then becomes the catalyst by which many seek a permanent estrangement—divorce. The kids want a divorce from the parents because the parents didn't treat them right. The business partner wants the other to drop dead because he doesn't do things the way the first partner wishes things to be done. The husband wants a new wife, and the wife says she wants a real man who will adore her and treat her right.

Unfortunately, what most individuals fail to realize is that becoming estranged in a relationship is, in fact, not the other person's fault, but is a self-perpetuating cycle that they themselves have initiated. If the young married couple would have actually taken the time to get premarital counseling, seek advice from couples married for preferably the same number of years that they are old, or spent time seriously getting to know themselves and being objective about all the things they observed about their potential spouse, many would not be married now. If the husband and wife would actually schedule time to be together in prayer for at least one hour a week, they would find that their hearts, thoughts, and desires would be intricately woven into one. And, when children approach their parents and are shunned or treated as a slave to be summoned only when the master beckons, what do you expect?

> Be not deceived; God is not mocked: for whatsoever a
> man soweth, that shall he also reap. For he that soweth
> to his flesh shall of the flesh reap corruption; but he that
> **soweth to the Spirit shall of the Spirit reap life**
> **everlasting** (Galatians 6:7-8).

Painful though it may be, when relationships become estranged for whatever the reasons, ultimately it can be traced back to a decision that each and every one of us has made personally. Be it a decision to place something or someone (especially our own personal desires) above that of someone else,

or just not heeding the warnings and promptings of the Holy
Spirit about a situation or proposed course of action, it will
inevitably be reduced down to a choice that each individual
makes.

The entire concept of estrangement then becomes the
backdrop to understanding what God is doing in the remainder
of this first chapter of Hosea. God is not giving Israel a bill of
divorce (Hosea 1:9) such as was instituted in Deuteronomy 24:1.

> When a man hath taken a wife, and married her, and it
> come to pass that she find no favour in his eyes, because
> he hath found some uncleanness in her: then let him
> write her a bill of divorcement, and give it in her hand,
> and send her out of his house.

For Jesus told the Pharisees that with regard to putting away
one's wife "for the hardness of your heart he [Moses] wrote you
this precept" (Deuteronomy 24:1), but "What therefore God
hath joined together, let not man put asunder" (Mark 10:2-9).
Note that Jesus said with regard to divorce, it was because of the
hardness of your heart. This is the self-perpetuating decision I
mentioned previously.

What God is issuing to them, to Israel, is a "bill of
estrangement." All situations in which people become estranged
are ultimately the result of violating two primary precepts:
intimacy (deep personal knowledge and fellowship) and
covenant relationships (be it by marital, contractual, verbal, or
family bonding). The LORD himself personally promised to
Abraham (Genesis 17:8b-9), Moses (Exodus 29:45), and others
such as the Prophet Jeremiah that He would:

Give them [Israel]: a heart to know me, that I am the LORD: and they shall be my people, and I will a be their God (Jeremiah 24:7).

But this thing commanded I them, saying, Obey my voice, and I will be your God, and ye shall be my people: and walk ye in all the ways that I have commanded you, that it may be well unto you (Jeremiah 7:23)

And they shall be my people, and I will be their God: And I will give them one heart, and one way, that they may fear me for ever, for the good of them, and of their children after them: And I will make an everlasting covenant with them, that I will not turn away from them, to do them good; but I will put my fear in their hearts, that they shall not depart from me. Yea, I will rejoice over them to do them good, and I will plant them in this land assuredly with my whole heart and with my whole soul (Jeremiah 32:38-41).

This is the covenant that the LORD pledged. This was the monogamous relationship to which Israel entered into with the LORD, one of intimacy, purpose, and promise. By entering into this divine relationship (covenant) with Israel, the LORD God was in effect "setting His name upon Israel," much in the same way a man's name is set upon (given unto) his wife at the time of their marriage, and inherited by their children. But like so many have done in their relationship with the LORD, or a spouse, a child, or others, Israel violated its covenant.

For so it was, that the children of Israel had sinned against the LORD their God, which had brought them up out of the land of Egypt, from under the hand of Pharaoh king of Egypt, and had feared [reverenced] other gods, And walked in the statutes of the heathen, whom the LORD cast out from before the children of Israel, and of the kings of Israel, which they had made.

And the children of Israel did secretly those things that were not right against the LORD their God, and they built them high places in all their cities, from the tower of the watchmen to the fenced city. And they set them up images and groves in every high hill, and under every green tree:

And there they burnt incense in all the high places, as did the heathen whom the LORD carried away before them; and wrought wicked things to provoke the LORD to anger: For they served idols, whereof the LORD had said unto them, Ye shall not do this thing.

Yet the LORD testified against Israel, and against Judah, by all the prophets, and by all the seers, saying, Turn ye from your evil ways, and keep my commandments and my statutes, according to all the law which I commanded your fathers, and which I sent to you by my servants the prophets.

Notwithstanding they would not hear, but hardened their necks, like to the neck of their fathers, that did not believe in the LORD their God (2 Kings 17:7-14).

Therefore, because of Israel's unrepentant disobedience, the LORD was forced into a position where HE declares "*Loammi*:

for ye are not my people, and I will not be your God" (Hosea 1:9). It is not merely a problem with Israel breaking vows or covenant with the LORD that spawns this response, but also at issue is the Lord's very nature. "God is light, and in him is no darkness at all" (John 1:5b). Those who would be in intimate (really personal knowing or deep understanding) relationship with Him must be Holy as He is Holy (Leviticus 11:45b). The LORD then, by His very nature, can have nothing to do in any way, shape, or fashion with sin:

> For what fellowship hath righteousness with unrighteousness? And what communion hath light with darkness? And what concord hath Christ with Belial? Or what part hath he that believeth with an infidel? And what agreement hath the temple of God with idols? (2 Corinthians 6:14b – 16a)

Israel, as a nation, was participating in practices which were totally contrary to the very nature, the very essence of who and what the LORD is. Were the LORD to continue to be associated in intimate fellowship with Israel on their terms, He would in effect cease to be God, which is something that He cannot do.

> Therefore will I do unto this house [Israel], which is called by my name, wherein ye trust, and unto the place that I gave to you and to your fathers, as I have done to Shiloh. And I will cast you out of my sight (Jeremiah 7:14-15).

The proclamation "*Loammi*," meaning "not my people," was not therefore a putting away of one's covenant partner, as in divorce, but a statement to the world by the LORD that He was no longer in fellowship with (agreement, harmony, or leadership of) Israel, and that the rights and privileges that came from being associated with **His name had been suspended, but not revoked!** They had become, in effect, estranged from one another.

Remember, however, just because something is suspended, or someone estranged, you are not necessarily relieved of the obligations concerning the remainder of the covenant relationship. Parents, though they may ground their children for disobedience, still are not relieved of their covenant rights to care for them. Criminals, though they violate the law in the gravest of situations, still have rights to protection, trials, and due process under the law. Leaders or officials, though they may violate their oaths of office, still are due a certain level of respect that is afforded them because of their legal position. Just because one party to a covenant relationship violates the terms of the agreement, it does not preclude, nullify, or void the other party's obligation to uphold it.

By that same token, those who violate contracts or break covenant with someone, not only are they subject to lose all of the rights and benefits of that covenant relationship, but they also now become totally responsible for dealing with all the consequences of their actions. Remember, it's a personal choice; **it is always the decision of your own choosing whenever you decide to break covenant.**

God, though issuing Israel a "declaration of estrangement," still intends, however, to honor the covenants He made with His servants Abraham, Isaac, Jacob, Moses, David, and many others. This is why the message of hope and restoration was given in verses 10-11 of Hosea, Chapter One.

¹²Yet the number of the children of Israel shall be as the sand of the sea, which cannot be measured nor numbered; and it shall come to pass, that in the place where it was said unto them, Ye are not my people, there it shall be said unto them, Ye are the sons of the living God.

¹³Then shall the children of Judah and the children of Israel be gathered together, and appoint themselves one head, and they shall come up out of the land: for great shall be the day of Jezreel.

The God of Abraham, Isaac, and Jacob had promised that from out of Abraham's loins would come a nation and descendants that numbered like the sands of the sea and stars of the sky, and through this seed all the nations of the earth shall be blessed (Genesis 22:15-18). To His faithful servant Moses, the LORD covenanted that the children of Israel would not only enter into, but would also possess "The Promised Land"—a land truly flowing with milk and honey (Leviticus 20:1,24). And to King David, a man after His own heart (Acts 13:22), the LORD promised that his throne should be established before Him forever (1 Kings 2:45).

So it is then, that in these final two verses of Chapter One of Hosea, we see a covenant—keeping God, who despite the heartache of tough love and the pain of estrangement, still remains faithful to His Word, His covenants, and His people.

Jesus Christ, the same, yesterday, and forever. For I am the LORD, I change not! (Hebrews 13:8, Malachi 3:6).

CHAPTER SIX
Violation and Atrocity

Say ye unto your brethren, *Ammi* [my people]; and to your sisters, *Ruhamah* [my pitied or loved ones].

² Plead with your mother, plead: for she is not my wife, neither am I her husband: let her therefore put away her whoredoms out of her sight, and her adulteries from between her breasts;

³ Lest I strip her naked, and set her as in the day that she was born, and make her as a wilderness, and set her like a dry land, and slay her with thirst.

⁴ And I will not have mercy upon her children; for they be the children of whoredoms.

⁵ For their mother hath played the harlot: she that conceived them hath done shamefully: for she said, I will go after my lovers, that give me my bread and my water, my wool and my flax, mine oil and my drink.

[6] Therefore, behold, I will hedge up thy way with thorns, and make a wall, that she shall not find her paths.

[7] And she shall follow after her lovers, but she shall not overtake them; and she shall seek them, but shall not find them: then shall she say, I will go and return to my first husband; for then was it better with me than now.

[8] For she did not know that I gave her corn, and wine, and oil, and multiplied her silver and gold, which they prepared for Baal.

[9] Therefore will I return, and take away my corn in the time thereof, and my wine in the season thereof, and will recover my wool and my flax given to cover her nakedness.

[10] And now will I discover her lewdness in the sight of her lovers, and none shall deliver her out of mine hand.

[11] I will also cause all her mirth to cease, her feast days, her new moons, and her Sabbaths, and all her solemn feasts.

[12] And I will destroy her vines and her fig trees, whereof she hath said, These are my rewards that my lovers have given me: and I will make them a forest, and the beasts of the field shall eat them.

[13] And I will visit upon her the days of Baalim, wherein she burned incense to them, and she decked herself with her earrings and her jewels, and she went after her lovers, and forgat me, saith the LORD (Hosea 2:1-13)

As I read through this section of Hosea, I became overwhelmed with the many images and faces of people whose lives lay in ruins. Hopes, dreams, desires, visions, and plans for a future in the Lord, all with the life sucked out of them as they lay at the foot of some precipice floundering amongst the rocks; scuttled, hollowed, and shipwrecked. In case you haven't figured out to what I am referring, let me be clear. I am referring to the atrocities and violations committed against the victims of divorce or legal separation: the children, congregations, and all of the people within an individual's sphere of influence.

I have, on several occasions, had the opportunity and pleasure to discuss issues involving organizational growth and influence with various learned colleagues of mine in academia, and it really did come as a bit of a surprise to me to learn that every individual has a sphere of influence of some 250+ people directly and indirectly, whether they know it or not. This means that the decisions every individual makes on a routine basis will have consequences or repercussions, whether they be good or bad, in more lives then just their own, especially their children. Sadly, I must admit that within my own sphere of influence, I have been touched by and been asked to advise people who were casualties of divorce or legal separation. The lie from the pit of hell that "the grass is greener on the other side" is just that—a lie from the pit of hell. The truth is:

> Be not deceived; God is not mocked: for whatsoever a man soweth, that shall he also reap. For he that soweth to his flesh shall of the flesh reap corruption; but he that soweth to the Spirit shall of the Spirit reap life everlasting (Galatians 6:7-8).

Whatever lessons you do not learn, whatever hurdles you do not overcome in your present marriage, will have to be addressed in the next one, without fail. Unfortunately, many do not realize this (or just don't want to hear it), and make shipwreck of their lives, and many others. Proverbs 4:7 says: "Wisdom is the principal thing; therefore get wisdom: and with all thy getting get understanding." Lest, according to 2 Corinthians 2:11: "Satan should get an advantage of us: for we are not ignorant of his devices."

Hosea 4:6 says: "My people are destroyed for lack of knowledge: because thou hast rejected knowledge..."

People who contemplate divorce or separation (except for the purpose of reconciliation) not only are missing the mark, but also oftentimes sin against their own body. It is this lack of knowledge, this ignorance that not only leads to sin, but devastation to all those within your sphere of influence, that the LORD is addressing in Hosea Chapter Two.

In verse one we see the Lord calling upon "*Ammi*" and "*Ruhamah*," which are obvious references to the children of Hosea and Gomer, as well as their brethren. This word "brethren" is "*ach*" in the Hebrew, meaning a brother, relative, or family within the widest possible sense of the word. In other words, the LORD is also referring to the people who are being influenced by the actions of this couple (their sphere of influence). What does the LORD tell them? "Plead with your mother, plead."

In Hebrew literature, anytime a word is mentioned twice within a sentence or phrase, a double emphasis is immediately placed upon that word. The first mentioning of the word sets the precedence or tone for the situation; the second occurrence of the word puts extreme urgency or emphasis on it; and three times means that it is considered to be the highest form of truth. So in verse two, the LORD is telling Hosea to plead (contend with, complain to, debate, rebuke, grapple with, and wrangle) with literally the mother of his children, and figuratively, Israel the nation. Do whatever it takes to convince her to "put away her whoredoms out of her sight, and her adulteries from between her breasts."

Apparently, Gomer, now the wife of the preacher Hosea, had decided to return to her ways as a cult or temple prostitute (the-grass-is-greener-on-the-other-side syndrome). Now having done so, her husband Hosea, and their children, found out about her life, once again as a temple prostitute. This is what provoked the stern warning and plea to Gomer from her family, and symbolically of God to Israel as a nation. True to His nature and convent, the LORD also discloses to Gomer (also representative of Israel) the consequences of her behavior if she does not repent. The LORD will: "Strip her naked, and set her as in the day that she was born, and make her as a wilderness, and set her like a dry land, and slay her with thirst."

While perhaps somewhat literal, what the LORD is really saying is that He will allow the entire truth to be known about Gomer, cut off her resources, and allow her to be used until she is basically a dried-up shell of what she was or could have been. The LORD will allow Gomer to be shown for who and what she really is.

One of the tragedies of a separation or divorce proceeding is that everything you never wanted anyone to know becomes public information. In America, unless a special dispensation is granted, most legal matters, wills, divorces, separations, child custody battles, et cetera, become a matter of public information. Anyone can get a copy of this information and is free to disseminate it. Answers to questions such as:

- How many divorces have you had?
- Have you ever been arrested, if so, for what reason(s)?
- How many abortions have you had?

♦ Drug convictions, instances of mental illness, prostitution convictions, and murder?

♦ Which sexually transmitted diseases have you tested positive for?

♦ The full names of all of the lovers you have ever had, and the manner in which any or all of your sexual contacts with these people were performed.

All of this is revealed in the course of securing a legal separation or divorce. Some people such as presidents, dignitaries, government officials, pastors, teachers, evangelists, and powerful people of influence never recover from the scandals of these types of proceedings, or the nakedness of their lives that is permanently exposed to the public at large. One could very well find all of their personal, private, and intimate information posted on someone's website. While unfortunate, this is the reality of the decisions that people enter into when they seek these types of proceedings. So much personal energy, so many resources and so many lives torn apart over one decision, especially where children are involved.

Of all of the unfortunate casualties of separations such as the relatives, friends, extended family, and congregations, my heart goes out the most to the children involved. For it is they who must endure all of the violations and atrocities for generations to come. They live with the emotional, psychological, physiological, and destructive venom that is spewed when relationships are allowed to sour. The effects of the decisions made during a separation or legal proceeding always have long-term, even generational, consequences. Be sure your sins will find you out: "For **the iniquity of the parents is visited upon** [affects] **the children, and upon the children's children, unto the third and to the fourth generation**" (Exodus 34:7). It is because of this very danger of generational curses and ramifications that it is said of the Lord in the Gospel of Mark:

> But when Jesus saw it, he was much displeased, and said unto them, "Suffer the little children to come unto me, and forbid them not: for of such is the kingdom of God" (Mark 10:14).

> And whosoever shall offend one of these little ones that believe in me, it is better for him that a millstone were hanged about his neck, and he were cast into the sea (Mark 9:42).

It is apparent that GOD takes the situation of these violated ones quite seriously, and so should the parents.

Once, I had the opportunity to speak with a couple that we shall call Carl and Lorraine. They were your typical middle-class family, middle-class values, attended a great church, and had children. As the story goes, they had been married for somewhere between eight and ten years, and from all outward appearances things seemed to be fine. One day Lorraine announced to her husband that she was pregnant and expecting their next child, and that's when things began to unravel. Apparently, she and her husband had separated for several months and had reconciled; however, the due date for the baby placed the date of conception a week or so prior to the date they had reconciled. At issue was whether or not the child was actually Carl's. As most of you may know, due dates and conception dates are not an exact science. The doctor can be off on either one, by as much as two to four weeks or more. This issue led to some very serious questions for Lorraine from her husband. She finally had to concede that she had in fact had an extra-marital affair with someone she once knew during their time of separation. The result—Hosea 2:4-6:

> I will not have mercy upon her children; for they be the
> children of whoredoms. For their mother hath played
> the harlot: she that conceived them hath done
> shamefully: for she said, I will go after my lovers, that
> give me my bread and my water [food], my wool and my
> flax [clothing and material needs], mine oil and my drink
> [medical care]. Therefore, behold, I will hedge up thy
> way with thorns, and make a wall, that she shall not find
> her paths.

Carl left! He wanted nothing to do with her, the child she was carrying, and even became suspicious of whether the children they had were actually his. He, except for the King James Version dialect of the Scriptures, expressed to her everything listed in these several verses of Hosea 2:4-6. He cut her and the children off completely. No money for the rent, no food supplies, took the automobile, and moved in with his parents. So who suffered the most for her indiscretions, and his reaction? **Their children suffered**. These children, who had been raised in a very stable home, now became the casualties of the indiscretions of their mother.

Carl and Lorraine managed to piece back together their marriage after several more months of separation and healing, and all appeared fine until about two or three years later when Carl, to my dismay, discovered his wife had never actually terminated her adulterous relationship and had been intimate with this particular individual on numerous occasions. Regretfully, the relationship ended in divorce. The real atrocity, however, came later when the children were forced to try and cope with their new living situations and the offenses perpetrated upon them in the name-calling and message passing that their parents used them for.

Also, I feel it noteworthy to mention that, although one of their children was from an adulterous relationship, Carl still took the child to be his own, even unto the giving of his last name to it. He never mentioned to anyone, not even this cute little one, that the child was not biologically his. Unfortunately, around the child's seventh birthday, the oldest child overhead a privileged conversation of his mother's and discovered the truth about his younger sibling's birthright. As big brothers will do, he began to tease his younger sibling about having a different father. Eventually, the children's mother heard about this and had to, now years later, continue to deal with the consequences of her action. On the one hand, she had to acknowledge to the younger child and ask for forgiveness for not telling them the truth concerning the child's real father. As for the oldest sibling who was doing the teasing, she only said to him out of frustration and humiliation: "Yes, I'm the one who played the whore! So if you really have something to say, say it to my face!"

While I appreciate the direct approach as much as anyone else, sometimes one can be just a bit abrupt. This might have been one of those occasions, and yet this clearly illustrates what God is saying, whether to Carl and Lorraine or Gomer—no one has to pay the price for a parent's action more than children. It is they who have to daily live in the ruins of permanent separations, affairs, and **selfishness instead of selflessness**. I am convinced that if more parents had to truly answer to their own children in total honesty about their relationships, there would be fewer divorces or separations in this country, such as Carl and Lorraine's or of another couple I dealt with whom we shall call Matthew and Carol.

Matthew and Carol's story, while not similar to Carl and

Lorraine's, does precisely parallel verses seven through thirteen of Hosea Chapter 2:

> [7]And she shall follow after her lovers, but she shall not overtake them; and she shall seek them, but shall not find them: then shall she say, I will go and return to my first husband; for then was it better with me than now.

> [8]For she did not know that I gave her corn, and wine, and oil, and multiplied her silver and gold, which they prepared for Baal.

> [9]Therefore will I return, and take away my corn in the time thereof, and my wine in the season thereof, and will recover my wool and my flax given to cover her nakedness.

> [10]And now will I discover her lewdness in the sight of her lovers, and none shall deliver her out of mine hand.

> [11]I will also cause all her mirth to cease, her feast days, her new moons, and her Sabbaths, and all her solemn feasts

> [12]And I will destroy her vines and her fig trees, whereof she hath said, These are my rewards that my lovers have given me: and I will make them a forest, and the beasts of the field shall eat them.

> [13]And I will visit upon her the days of *Baalim*, wherein she burned incense to them, and she decked herself with her earrings and her jewels, and she went after her lovers, and forgat me, saith the LORD.

Carol had taken the children one day while Matt was at work and had seemingly left, leaving no note, no explanation, nothing. The only reason that Matt and the authorities ruled out a possible kidnapping was because half of Carol's clothing was gone, along with much of the children's. Apparently, after I found Carol and was able to talk with her, things had not been going well between her and Matt for better than a year. Instead of talking about it with each other, they mainly tried to cover over or whitewash the issues. They both had allowed seeds of bitterness to crop up, which in turn grew and began strangling their marital relationship. She used him for money and the necessities of life, all the while, he utilized her to convenience his desires.

Several months prior to their separation, an old boyfriend (lover) of Carol's called her up and the two began to talk, primarily when her husband Matthew wasn't around. After Carol's disappearance, several of Matthew's friends and colleagues told him that they had spotted his wife and children driving along the interstate in one of their cars, but that some man was actually doing all of the driving. It turns out that this man was none other than Carol's former lover. This was now the situation that they both found themselves in, as well as their children!

When I asked Carol where she and the children had been staying, she rather sheepishly told me that she and her friend had been spending weekends together in some of the local hotels, but she always had the children in an adjourning bedroom; the remainder of the week, she and the children stayed with one of her divorced friends. The days turned into weeks, and the weeks into months. Matthew, during those periods, aggressively tried to meet with, date, and even work out some type of truce whereby their marriage might be reconciled. Finally fed up with Carol's indecisiveness, her unwillingness to permanently let go of her lover, and the rumors he had heard that she had been consulting an attorney (in order to secure temporary maintenance, the family residence, and child support), filed for a separation.

Once again, during all of this, who were the victims of the atrocities? The children and all of the people in both their spheres of influence became the casualties. Family members found themselves eventually taking sides. The children wanted both parents together, but found themselves bitterly torn between which parents they might end up with. The friends and acquaintances who looked upon this family as a model from the Lord of what their own could be like, began to stumble and falter, and both sides refused good solid counseling.

Finally the day came for a temporary hearing on the "bill of estrangement" (separation) that Matthew had filed. Matthew had actually filed for a separation, which left open the possibilities of reconciliation without any stipulations toward a divorce, but I am sorry to say that Carol had asked for a full-blown divorce. The judge elected to grant a temporary separation, pending further legal discovery. In the interim, Carol was left with her lover, the children, and no court-ordered support from Matthew until they returned to court in six months. It did please me to know that up until the day of the ruling by the judge, Matthew had actually made arrangements to give Carol some money for food and other expenses for the children along the way, all with the anticipation of her returning home.

Having heard the judge's temporary decision, Carol became extremely upset and left the courtroom in a fury. I believe it was at that moment that the wisdom of Hosea 2:7-12 actually became real to her. Her lover, while using her body and allowing her to spend the money she had, hadn't really spent much money on her, nor tried to help her with her children. Sure, he may have bought her children a couple of pizza dinners, or given her flowers, a night out with dinner and a few cards, but nothing of real substance. All that she had ever really had came from her husband, and now those securities were removed.

As a side note, Carol's lover showed his real intentions when he found out that she had received no type of support that day in court. He told her, while he wished he were in a position to help her and her children out, he really couldn't afford to give her much in the way of support, as he was still living with his relatives.

So reluctantly Carol called Matt and suggested maybe, perhaps, they could reconcile or work something out for the betterment of all, but it would have to be on her terms, and he would have to make separate financial arrangements for her. Unfortunately for Carol, this was not well received by her husband or her lover, and she found herself metaphorically speaking "in a wilderness—naked, bare, alone, and ashamed." The little that she had had, including her wedding ring, had been spent pursuing her lover, the attorney, and pleasures. The only thing worse than this was that her own children literally reminded her that it was because of her decision to leave that they were all in that current situation. While children may not always have all of the answers, they are extremely perceptive, and have a God-given way of crystallizing certain things for adults.

Make no mistake about it; legal separations or divorces are cruel, brutal, savage, and the consequences extremely deceptive. No one wins ultimately, and everyone involved or within your sphere of influence becomes a casualty, especially the children. If you are contemplating divorce, separation, or have contemplated or entered into an affair I say to you, according to Romans 5:19-6:2:

Rom 5:19—For as by one man's disobedience many were made sinners, so by the obedience of one shall many be made righteous. [If you have messed up, it may not be too late to make things right, and there is nothing so horrible that God Himself is not willing to work with you on it.]

Rom 5:20—Moreover the law entered, that the offence might abound. But where sin abounded, grace did much more abound. [Even if you have started legal proceedings, through counseling, patience, and selflessness in Christ, one can still stop those legal proceedings and right the wrongs, hurts, and destructiveness. To the degree you show forgiveness and mercy, is to the degree and manner in which God will allow it to be shown unto you.]

Rom 5:21—That as sin hath reigned unto death, even so might grace reign through righteousness unto eternal life by Jesus Christ our Lord. [Although one or both parties may be guilty of atrocities against the other, there is nothing that unconditional love and the grace (mercy) of God cannot overcome.]

Rom 6:1-2 - What shall we say then? Shall we continue in sin, that grace may abound? God forbid. How shall we, that are dead to sin, live any longer therein? [Suspending legal proceedings or attempting to give someone a second chance in the relationship does not make you weak, but in fact makes you stronger as long as it is done with humility and, if need be, using tough love.]

For:

He said unto me, My grace is sufficient for thee: for my strength is made perfect in weakness. Most gladly therefore will I rather glory in my infirmities, that the power of Christ may rest upon me (2 Corinthians 12:9).

Therefore I take pleasure in infirmities, in reproaches, in necessities, in persecutions, in distresses for Christ's sake: for when I am weak, then am I strong (2 Corinthians 12:10).

Remember, no one wins ultimately in situations involving divorce or legal separation, and everyone involved or within your sphere of influence becomes a casualty, especially your children.

Chapter Seven
The Road to Restoration and Reconciliation

[14] Therefore, behold, I will allure her, and bring her into the wilderness, and speak comfortably unto her.

[15] And I will give her her vineyards from thence, and the valley of Achor for a door of hope: and she shall sing there, as in the days of her youth, and as in the day when she came up out of the land of Egypt.

[16] And it shall be at that day, saith the LORD, that thou shalt call me Ishi [my husband]; and shalt call me no more *Baali* [my master].

[17] For I will take away the names of *Baalim* [false gods] out of her mouth, and they shall no more be remembered by their name.

¹⁸ And in that day will I make a covenant for them with the beasts of the field, and with the fowls of heaven, and with the creeping things of the ground: and I will break the bow and the sword and the battle out of the earth, and will make them to lie down safely.

¹⁹ And I will betroth thee unto me forever; yea, I will betroth thee unto me in righteousness, and in judgment, and in loving kindness, and in mercies.

²⁰ I will even betroth thee unto me in faithfulness: and thou shalt know the LORD.

²¹ And it shall come to pass in that day, I will hear, saith the LORD, I will hear the heavens, and they shall hear the earth;

²² And the earth shall hear the corn, and the wine, and the oil; and they shall hear *Jezreel*.

²³ And I will sow her unto me in the earth; and I will have mercy upon her that had not obtained mercy; and I will say to them which were not my people, Thou art my people; and they shall say, Thou art my God. (Hosea 2:14-23)

About five to ten years ago, my wife and I happened to be at the home of a very close friend. We had just finished a rather large dinner as I recall, and afterwards were reclining in the living room discussing various topics. As his wife passed by, he mentioned that their anniversary was coming up soon. Having never really thought about it, I asked him which one was coming up, and it was then that he said something that totally took me by surprise. What he said was that he wasn't actually sure, depending on from which point you calculated the start of their marriage. Rather confused and a bit taken back, I asked him to explain. This was to me, and has remained, one of the best examples of Hosea 2:14-23 that I have ever heard.

Out of respect for their personal privacy, I will refer to my friends as Jason, and his wife as Maria.

About seven or eight years prior, Jason and Maria had decided to renew their wedding vows in a small church in the town where they both had grown up. What made this renewing of vows so monumental was the fact that they were doing it after having been divorced for several years. Their first attempt at marriage with each other had ended tragically in divorce, and left their daughter's life in a state of real chaos. Jason had started turning to drugs to compensate for what he deemed rejection and depression, while Maria became aggressive, and to quote her, downright mean toward certain men, especially her former husband. After about a year and a half of weekends with his daughter, and watching his former wife out with other men, Jason went to the one person he had never asked for help—God!

As Jason gradually surrendered his life to the Lord, the Lord began to reveal to him a plan by which he could not only continue his healing process, but also effect reconciliation in his relationship with his Maria as well. "For the LORD hates divorce" (Mark 10:2-12). What Jason basically did was to apply the principles of reconciliation found in Hosea 2:14-23. "Therefore, behold, I will allure [to be roomy, flatter, or persuade] her, and bring her into the wilderness [symbolic of being alone or isolated], and speak comfortably unto her" (Hosea 2:14).

Jason began by giving Maria her own personal space. Instead of seeking every opportunity to try and see her or be near her, he basically left her alone. No unnecessary phone calls, no messages sent to her by their daughter, no legal actions, no questions concerning who she might be dating—nothing. Next, whenever Jason would see Maria during their periods for child custody exchange, he made a conscious effort to always smile at her, and when she had on a new outfit or hairstyle, to compliment her with just a few simple words of praise, then leave.

Proverbs 10:19 says: "In the multitude of words there wanteth not sin: but he that refraineth his lips is wise." In other words, if he didn't say much, he couldn't get into trouble or possibly start an argument with her (Proverbs 17:28).

At the same time, he was sowing seed into the life of his former wife. Jason spent a lot of time rebuilding a heart that sought after God, allowing the Holy Spirit to reveal to him, work on, and eliminate his own personal shortcomings in his thinking that had resulted in the dissolution of his first marriage. Finally Jason allowed the Lord to give him a "heart transplant" as he studied Scriptures to **rebuild a clear conscience that yields a forgiving spirit**. All of this wasn't overnight, but over a course of more than a year and a half. Then suddenly, one compliment led to a "can you stay for a moment?" "Can you stay for a moment?" gave way to "Would you like to meet me for lunch at school with our daughter for Parent's Day?" During these gradual increases, there were times of testing also—but not by Maria, and definitely not by God: "Let no man say when he is tempted, I am tempted of God: for God cannot be tempted with evil, neither tempteth he any man."

These times of testing were actually carefully laid traps laid by Satan and Jason's own flesh to try and abort if possible, derail at a minimum, what God was gradually cultivating. For Jason, one of the tests was the temptation to accelerate God's plan by promoting his plans. "But every man is tempted, when he is drawn away of his own lust, and enticed" (James 1:13-14).

But, praise be to God, Jason stayed submitted to the Holy Spirit, and prevailed in the end against:

♦ Old boyfriends showing up or dropping by. All Jason would do is excuse himself without any hints of annoyance and go home.

♦ Seeing Maria in public talking to some gentlemen. Jason's response was simply a smile, a subtle nod of acknowledgment in her general direction and he went on about his business.

No coming up to Maria, no confrontations, no demands for an explanation later—nothing. Jason acted as though none of these things happened. The end result after an extended period of time was:

And I will give her her vineyards from thence, and the valley of Achor for a door of hope: and she shall sing there, as in the days of her youth, and as in the day when she came up out of the land of Egypt (Hosea 2:15).

Jason and Maria began dating again. Nothing hurried, nothing forced, just enjoying each other's company and true friendship. Finally, when the Holy Spirit said it was right, not Jason, he asked Maria for an opportunity to make right the previous wrongs of their marriage. To his utter amazement, Maria accepted his proposal.

"And it shall be at that day, saith the LORD, that thou shalt call me *Ishi* [my husband]" (Hosea 2:16a).

On advice from the Holy Spirit, Jason, to this day, has never mentioned one time, to my knowledge, anything to Maria about any former boyfriends. "For I will take away the names of *Baalim* [false gods or former lovers] out of her mouth, and they shall no more be remembered by their name" (Hosea 2:17).

Several months later, with the past behind them, Jason and Maria remarried—"and in that day will I make a covenant" (Hosea 2:18). The vows Jason exchanged with his new wife Maria were ones similar to Hosea 2:19-23, for just as the LORD had been dealing with Jason, he had also been dealing with Maria on issues in her life.

♦ And I will betroth thee unto me forever [never allowing divorce to be an option again];

♦ Yea, I will betroth thee unto me in righteousness [right standing with and fully submitted to God],

♦ And in judgment [having a clear conscience and a pure heart before God],

♦ And in loving-kindness, and in mercies [dealing with her according to knowledge, giving honor to the wife, as to the weaker vessel, and as being heirs together of the grace of life, that their prayers be not hindered].

♦ I will even betroth thee unto me in faithfulness [being fully committed to those things which will yield the highest possible Godly results in life for the other person, even at your own personal expense].

♦ And thou shalt know the LORD [purposing to use Godly wisdom, uphold Godly standards, to preach and teach by personal witness or living example, the Gospel of Jesus Christ].

I am happy to say, that to this day, Jason and Maria are the happiest of couples. Jason sought first the kingdom of God and all things (his heart's desires) were given to him (Matthew 6:33). If you need God's prescription for reconciliation, take notes from the lives of Jason and Maria. "**All things are possible to him that believeth.**"

The living testimony of Jason and Maria's lives together is, for me, a modern-day example of the principles and messages that the LORD was trying to speak to Israel through Hosea and Gomer. Because of Israel's infidelity to her covenant partner, the LORD had been continually humiliated. He was experiencing pain, suffering, and the heartache that comes from being rejected by the one He loved, to which end, Hosea the prophet, also willingly partook of this same suffering in his marriage to his wife Gomer. At the heart of this later half of Hosea Chapter Two is this one eternal message:

> Successful marriages are not the ones involving two perfect people (for there are no perfect people). Instead, marriage "is a state in which two very imperfect people often, whether accidentally or on purpose (to be blunt about it), hurt, offend, or even humiliate one another; yet nevertheless, they continue to reach out to each other with grace, forgiveness, and a compassion that brings the life-changing power of God into their mutual lives.

CHAPTER EIGHT
Fifteen Pieces of Silver

Then said the LORD unto me, Go yet, love a woman beloved of her friend, yet an adulteress, according to the love of the LORD toward the children of Israel, who look to other gods, and love flagons of wine. So I bought her to me for fifteen pieces of silver, and for an homer of barley, and an half-homer of barley (Hosea 3:1-2).

When I first read over this passage of Scripture, I could not help but be impressed and even placed in awe of just how much the LORD is communicating in this chapter. It is not just what it says, but also because of all the nuances, subtle meanings and inferences that the LORD has packed into these statements, that I never cease to be amazed at how relevant and alive the word of God truly is. These verses speak volumes about the heart of God! Allow me to demonstrate exactly what I mean.

Starting with verse one, here are the keys (words) that help to unlock the entire meaning of this chapter.

Verse One:

♦ **Go**: Pronounced *ya-lak* in the Hebrew—walk, carry away, bear (again), follow after, pursue, prosper, to be weak before.

♦ **Yet**: Pronounced *owd* in the Hebrew—continuance, henceforth, all life long.

♦ **Woman**: Pronounced *ish-shah* in the Hebrew—a woman as in an adulteress, an adulterer, wife, or woman.

♦ **Friend**: Pronounced *ray-ah* in Hebrew—a companion, lover, neighbor, husband, or paramour (person who is treated with all the rights of a spouse, but does not have the legal rights to do so because the individuals are not married)

♦ **Love** (the second occurrence): Pronounced *ahabah* in Hebrew—with the same amount or intensity of love as before.

♦ **Toward**: Pronounced *eth* in the Hebrew—nearness

♦ **Children**: Pronounced *ben* or *ba-ne* in the Hebrew—sons, offspring, a builder of a family name

♦ **Israel**: Pronounced *yis-raw-ale'* in Hebrew—He will rule with God

There are some things in life that are truly difficult. So much so that they are sometimes beyond the realm of human endurance, and well beyond the reach of some individuals, but "**with God all things are possible**" (Matthew 19:26), and so it is with unconditional love. What you have before you in verse one is the soul (mind, will, emotions, decision making) and the natural outpouring of the Father's love toward His people. This, too, is a heart that the Lord expects of all of those who claim to follow and serve Him. Many Bible scholars will tell you that there are three ways to know the will of God. You will always find God's perfect will for your life illustrated in the Garden of Eden, the life of Jesus, or His word. So what is the perfect will of God for Hosea as demonstrated in the first verses of chapter three?

And then the LORD said unto me, Go after, pursue, make yourself weak before your spouse ["when I am weak, then am I strong"(2 Corinthians 12:2)],

and I will prosper you [prosper meaning empowering to succeed], henceforth and all your life long, love an adulteress woman sexually involved with her friend and paramours, with the same love, commitment, devotion, and loyalty that the LORD does,

with the same nearness and tenderness as before [just like the LORD does] toward the children [builders of the family name and offspring, which demonstrates a solid relationship and committal of God towards all of mankind] of Israel [the ones who will rule as God does, who looks to other gods representing people, places or things] and love flagons of wine [literally raisin cake offerings, representative of sacrificial meal].

No matter how bad the situation, no matter what they have done to you, God says love with the same or greater love than you did before, toward your wife, your children, your relatives, in-laws, outlaws, et cetera. The LORD hates divorce, plain and simple. Divorce from your spouse, divorce or estrangement from your children or family (people cut their children or relatives off all the time, refusing to have anything to do with them). The LORD says: "This is not my heart." He loves unconditionally and expects all who call upon the name of the Lord Jesus to do the same. No holding back, no revenge, no "I'll show you or make you wish you had never hurt me." God is a father who believes in complete or full restoration and He not only forgives, but He forgets! And:

> Though I speak with the tongues of men and of angels, and have not love, I am become as sounding brass, or a tinkling cymbal.

> And though I have the gift of prophecy, and understand all mysteries, and all knowledge; and though I have all faith, so that I could remove mountains, and have not love, I am nothing.

> And though I bestow all my goods to feed the poor, and though I give my body to be burned, and have not love, it profiteth me nothing.

> Love suffereth long, and is kind; love envieth not; love vaunteth not itself, is not puffed up,

> Doth not behave itself unseemly, seeketh not her own, is not easily provoked, thinketh no evil;

Rejoiceth not in iniquity, but rejoiceth in the truth;

Beareth all things, believeth all things, hopeth all things, endureth all things.

Love never faileth (1 Corinthians 13:1-8)

So, Hosea went down to the slave market or local pimp, and purchased his own wife back from them for "fifteen pieces of silver, and for an homer of barley, and an half-homer of barley." In Hosea's time, the price of a decent slave was 30 pieces of silver (6-10 oz. or $0.64 U.S. per piece. In today's market about $120 U.S.). Hosea negotiated a price of about $72 in cash and barley grain (five bushels per homer) to redeem his wife from the slavery into which her sins had led her.

How much does unconditional love, love someone else? It loves them unconditionally. Imagine having to go to a public auction or to someone else to ask how much it will cost you for the freedom of the one you love. Keep in mind that if Gomer was at a local slave market, most slaves, even females, were paraded around with next to nothing on so that they could be inspected like cattle. For women, often times topless and rather out of it, like an addict that is strung out on drugs. Mangled or mangy, probably not having had a bath in weeks, bound in chains or shackles. Everyone knows who you are as a person of God, and knows this person you are attempting to buy back out of bondage.

Now fast forward this to the 21st century to a world in which, on the African continent, missionaries and others are still buying people out of slavery for about $1000 each. Little children are purchased from kiddy porn kings by pedophiles for about $500 here in America or abroad, people making payments to the leaders of street gangs in order for young kids (children, teens, young adults) to be allowed to leave alive, instead of butchered by their own sect for trying to leave that lifestyle. Sounds sad, but every day somewhere in the world, human beings, people who were created in the likeness and image of God, are sold for hard currency into or out of these living hells. How much does unconditional love, love? It loves enough to set the captives free, make the wounded whole, give rest through a saving knowledge of Jesus to the weary soul, to love totally, and forgive completely. In short, it loves unconditionally.

"And [Hosea] said unto her [Gomer], Thou shalt abide for me many days; thou shalt not play the harlot, and thou shalt not be for another man: so will I also be for thee" (Hosea 3:3 KJV).

So Hosea loved Gomer in the same manner and fashion as God loves us, and we should love others. He did not scold her and tell her what a whore she was. He did not tell her "if you ever do this thing again, that's it! I'm finished with you forever." No "look at you, you're such a mess," even though she probably really was in very bad shape. Instead of messages of criticism, despair, or humiliation, we see the prophet Hosea walking out what appears to be a four-step process on how to receive a prodigal, runaway, rebellious, or estranged love one back into the home. Hosea starts by echoing the heart of God the Father, the words of Jesus, and ministry of the Holy Spirit with a soft voice, a gentle touch, and his arms around her:

♦ I want you to come back home and stay [Step 1— Reconciliation, restoration, and hope is being infused into the relationship].

♦ I would like for you to give up that promiscuous [former] lifestyle, and not be intimate with any other man, especially former lovers [Step 2—Hosea is establishing a foundation on which the future of the relationship shall grow. He is letting Gomer know in a loving manner what the realistic goals and expectations will be once she is back in the home].

♦ I will in no wise cast you out" [Step 3—Assurance that no matter what, even if painful mistakes are made, they will not be given up on (John 6:37b KJV)].

♦ I will never leave thee, nor forsake thee" [Step 4— No matter what the final outcome, she will always be loved and you will do your very best to be there for them in the best possible way that benefits healing and restoration for both parties (Hebrews 13:5b – KJV)].

You see, love is not just a feeling, nor is it some schizophrenic psychotic force that possesses your soul (mind, will, emotions) at its leisure and departs when it pleases. No, true love *(agape*— Godly love) makes a conscious decision to love at all times, even if need be to its own hurt. It is a conscious decision to put the betterment of another individual above your own personal issues, pride, or social standing. Love is a now word, and an action verb. James the elder wrote, **"Faith without works is dead"** (James 2:20, 2:26). Well, so is love. Real love is not passive; it is always active, and very much involved, even when it seems to be silent, in prayer, or prolonged in its actions.

For the children of Israel shall abide many days without a king, and without a prince, and without a sacrifice, and without an image, and without an *ephod*, and without *teraphim*. Afterward shall the children of Israel return, and seek the LORD their God, and David their king; and shall fear the LORD and his goodness in the latter days (Hosea 3:4-5).

The story of Hosea's love now transcends in these final two verses of Chapter Three from the realm of the natural to that of the supernatural. "For the things which are seen are temporal; but the things which are not seen are eternal" (2 Corinthians 4:18). The events of your life are just physical or natural manifestations of what is or has already happened in the spiritual realm regarding your life. So just as Gomer had to be put away, so to speak, for a season so that she could undergo detoxification (liberation) from her former lifestyle in the natural realm, God in the spiritual was about to send Israel through detoxification that she might be made whole and reconciled unto Him in sweet intimacy. As part of God's detoxification of Israel from her pagan practices and lovers, He allowed the nation of Israel to experience the following:

♦ "For the children of Israel shall abide many days without a king." (King—symbolic of nationality or statehood.) Israel as a nation would be destroyed for a season and placed into exile. They would be without control of their promised land.

♦ "and without a prince" (Prince—symbolic of government, territorial authority.) Israel would not be able to govern itself once it was scattered or in exile. Others (strangers, foreigners, masters, leaders from other nations) would administrate or govern over these chosen people.

♦ "and without a sacrifice" (Sacrifice—symbolic of the covenant worship.) Israel would not be able to observe or practice their worship of the one true God in the places and at the times that God had ordained in the Book of Leviticus. Israel, as a covenant bride or nation, had taken the ability to worship (reverence and love) God for granted when going after other gods (demons spirits, material things, their own desires). It is as if someone had cheapened or defiled the marital bed by inviting others into bed simultaneously for an orgy. As such, not only was God not willing to share Israel with other gods, He wanted a new or purified bed (the bed here being representative of worship also).

♦ "and without an image" (Image—symbolic of cult practices and also direction.) Proverbs 29:18 says: **"Where there is no vision, the people perish."** If God were to allow Israel to be put in a situation whereby they could no longer have access to their pagan gods, they would eventually forget about them. You know the American expression "out of sight, out of mind." If something is not constantly in your view, if you are deprived of access to something, or it becomes beyond your ability to obtain, eventually you will adjust to being without it. Your way of living will change in order to compensate for its lost, in much the same way as a drug addict goes through withdrawal during detoxification. At first the person's body might ache, convulse, shake, or become extremely violent, but over time, it adjusts to not having the poison to which it was once addicted, and begins to settle down into a normal routine.

Often this is what happens in many marital

situations, or is revealed when counseling many parents about relationships with their children. You don't just "fall out of love," if it was ever true love to begin with, because love is an ongoing, conscious decision. It is an act of your will, and so is the decision to let go of the vision for the relationship also.

♦ "and without an *ephod*" (Ephod—symbolic of religion and man's attempt to come to God on his own terms.) An ephod was a priestly garment ordained by God in Exodus 28:6-12. It was also the very object that Gideon mistakenly created, which later became an idol, snare, and stumbling block for the children of Israel (Judges 8:27). What was meant by God to be a memorial or sign of His intimate relationship with Israel had now become a hindrance. So, too, oftentimes couples, when they are having marital problems or families are experiencing relationship problems, try to come to each other or relate to one another based upon their own unique set of terms, each wanting to maintain the upper hand and control the relationship. This not only does not work with people, but also is disastrous when approaching God.

God has set an order or prescribed manner to come to Him. Jesus said: "I am the way, the truth, and the life: no man cometh unto the Father, but by me" (John 14:6). You must come to God based on a relationship through Jesus, not your own conceived way. Any other manner is totally unacceptable by God. From an earthly perspective, when dealing with people, especially in a covenant relationship such as marriage, you must always reach out to the other person based on the way that ministers to them, not you! Never assume that what works for you or conveys love to you will also be interpreted the same way by your teenagers, children, or spouse, because it won't. That's why 1 Peter 3:7 was written: "Likewise, ye husbands, dwell with them according to knowledge, giving honour unto the wife, as unto the weaker vessel."

You deal with people based on where they are spiritually, emotionally, psychologically, and physically, not where you think they are or where they should be.

♦ "and without *teraphim*" (Teraphim—family or household gods made for use in worshipping one's ancestors). You know Jesus said in Luke 9:60, "Let the dead bury their dead," meaning let the spiritually dead bury the physically dead. Well, in the 21ˢᵗ century, with regard to unconditional love and walking out God's true love before others, often if you want your relationships to prosper, you will have to let go of many family traditions that did not yield positive fruit. If daddy beat up mommy, or mommy frequently disrespected daddy's authority, especially publicly, those old family gods or ancestral ways of doing things have to be cast out. Just because your relatives have always gone to this church, worshipped a particular way, or done the some old tired dead things, does not obligate you to do the same. To continue in those vain attempts will not only lead you into a rut, but possibly even to what many would define as insanity.

To do the same old tired things that produce the same old tired, inefficient, and unproductive results is the definition of and a life of perpetual insanity. Why would any sane, rational person do or use that which does not work or produce results for them? When companies do so, they find themselves quickly falling behind, down in market shares, and inevitably bankrupt or out of business. They cease to exist, and so it can be in your relationships if you are not careful.

Jesus was a radical for God. Dare to get out of the box or confines of your normal mundane world and do something for God, do something different for yourself. Dare to be different within the confines of God's Word (the Bible). That's not a limitation, but an invitation to experience life at its fullest. "I am come that they might have life, and that they might have it more abundantly" is what Jesus said in John 10:10.

Matthew 19:5 put it as "For this cause shall a man leave father and mother, and shall cleave to his wife: and they twain shall be one flesh!" Notice that it says the man leaves his parents and cleaves (bonds permanently with) his wife. This then is a new relationship, and as such may very well necessitate a departing from the old ways.

Throw off those old lifeless ways that didn't work for your ancestors. Embrace Jesus; worship God in His majesty according to the ways that He himself has placed in your heart. Dare to be radical for Christ, alive unto God, and bring fire, passion, love, intimacy, desire, and God's revelation into your relationships. Let the dead stay dead, and embrace life. Maximize every moment of your life, for "this is the day which the LORD hath made; we will rejoice and be glad" (Psalms 118:24).

As for (spiritual detoxification of Israel) the LORD says: "Afterward shall the children of Israel return, and seek the LORD their God, and David their king; and shall fear the LORD and his goodness in the latter days" (Hosea 3:5). This passage then becomes the climatic end to Chapter Three. Hope has been infused and given to Gomer to yet realize a very promising future despite personal failures or shortcomings. A promissory note regarding the future yet to be bestowed upon the bride Israel has been issued. For the prophet Hosea and his children, the season of restoration, harvest, and intimate fellowship has blossomed. What once was has now been forgiven, forgotten, and replaced with a life that is infinitely better. This is the promise and hope that Israel carries. A vision pronounced some three thousand years ago, now beginning to unfold as you read this passage. This is the vision of Israel, once scattered to the four corners of the globe, now called back to its promised land to be a nation once again, that all shall see the establishment of the Messiah and Deliverer (Jesus) as King, through which all the peoples of the earth shall fully experience the revelations and wonders of His love.

CHAPTER NINE
The Sins of the Fathers—
The Indictment

O n the day in which I wrote this chapter of the book, I was sitting in my office at home wondering what the Lord would have me write. It was during the Christmas holiday season and I began to think about one of my favorite holiday movies, *It's a Wonderful Life* starring Jimmy Stewart. Boy, do I like that movie. I like it so much I went out and bought it four or five years ago.

In the movie, Jimmy Stewart plays a character named George, who is left with or rather inherited the task of running his father's old savings and loan bank. When, through a brief mishap, the savings and loan comes up $5,000 short, he wishes he had never been born and an angel named Clarence grants him his wish. So for the next hour of the movie, George gets to see what everyone else in town's life would have been like had he never been born. His conclusion was that everyone else's life "sucked"—to be colloquial—or was worse because he had not been there at pivotal points in their lives. This leads George to the conclusion he wanted to be returned to his former life, because in all the things that really matter, his life was meaningful and wonderful. His was truly "a wonderful life."

In the life of every individual, every family, every society, God places key people who not only are there to help others, but also are human moral compasses for God. Their appointment, their calling, is to lead us toward calmer waters and into the safe harbor of God's arms. For some it was an elderly grandparent who took up the call of Abraham in their life when God said:

> For I know him, that he will command his children and his household after him, and they shall keep the way of the LORD, to do justice and judgment; that the LORD may bring upon Abraham that which he hath spoken of him (Genesis 18:19).

They told their children and their grandchildren, and everyone else's children about an awesome God who loved them, and could do anything, wasn't mad at them, but wanted to spend time with them in order to bless them. For others it could have been the elderly woman or teacher across the way that took you under her wing because God had placed in her heart the living New Testament that says "Be teachers of good things" (Titus 2:3).

Ideally, according to the word of God, in a home, this person should be the father. He is to be the spiritual leader, the moral compass for the household. Abraham fulfilled the role for his home, Moses was in his home, King David did for his home, and Jesus definitely did for his home after his earthly father Joseph died.

In my own life, my father was not around much for the first

twelve years of my life. Even before I was born again, God still looked out for me by placing people like Monsignor Bob or Mr. Jerry McGee in my life. Later it would be people such as Jansen Reynolds, Kenneth Matthews, Phillip White, and every little boy's natural superman, my father Willis (Proverbs 17:6—"**the glory of children are their fathers**"). Natural men, who made natural mistakes, and I fault none of them, neither does God, but that didn't stop them from being faithful in trying to keep me pointed in the right direction, especially through some extremely dark times in my life where Satan could have and probably made it his heart's desire for that day to try and take me out permanently.

God does this also for nations. In every generation God always sends men and women to help the leaders of society steer into calmer waters straight for the haven of the LORD. The ancients had Abraham, the Hebrew children in Egypt received Moses, and in modern times in America, there are men like the Reverend Billy Graham and Pope John Paul II. People who will not bow their knee or play word games, but speak God's uncompromised word, regardless of the circumstances. Unfortunately, as history has borne out again and again, depending on who is currently in power, these anointed men and women of God have often been without honor in their own lands. To quote Jesus himself in Mark 6:4: "A prophet is not without honour, but in his own country, and among his own kin, and in his own house."

When this happens, when the moral and spiritual leaders of a nation are not listened to, or worse, do not carry out the duties of the office that God has called them to, the results are always disastrous for the nation. One thing that contributes to the fall of a nation, its families, its people, is a failure to promote and lead by the word of God by the priesthood. While this does not relieve fathers and husbands of their duty before God to be the spiritual leader or moral compass before Him in their own homes, the absence of strong men and women who will stand up for God in their local communities leads to scandalous misfortunes in the lives of the citizens of a nation.

Wherever the church or spiritual leadership is quiet, nothing gets done spiritually, politically, or socially. **All that is necessary for evil and sin to exist and thrive is for good men to do nothing.** Many times, it is the lack of a presence of a strong Godly, God-fearing, God-seeking individual that causes the moral decay and decline of a nation or a household. A rise in crime is closely connected to violations of God's word. Without God, anything is possible in terms of vile atrocities. When people, especially children, are not taught God's word from an early age, they grow up to be rebellious violent adults. History has born this out with Sodom and Gomorrah (biblical archeologists now concede that these two biblical places were in actuality two very real cities), the early Roman Empire, and Nazi Germany, to name a few.

So how bad can it really get within a nation, or even within a family, you ask? Proverbs 29:18 (NIV) says: "Where there is no vision [revelation of God], the people perish [cast off all restraints]."

It got so bad in the prophet Hosea's land that the LORD Himself (The Self Existent One Who Reveals Himself) convened a spiritual tribunal and brought formal charges (legal indictments) against the people, the land, and the priest! (Hosea 4:1-19 – NIV):

THE INDICTMENT

Hear the word of the LORD, you Israelites, because the LORD has a charge [a legal indictment] to bring against you who live in the land

THE CHARGES (ALLEGATIONS) AGAINST THE PEOPLE

1. There is no faithfulness, no love, no acknowledgment of God in the land.

2. There is only cursing, lying and murder, stealing and adultery; they break all bounds [anything goes, if it feels good do it, nothing is sacred or off limits], and bloodshed follows bloodshed [people murdering others in order to gain revenge for murdered loved ones— vendettas, repeated gangbanging or drive-by shootings].

Because of this the land mourns, and all who live in it waste away; the beasts of the field and the birds of the air and the fish of the sea are dying (Verse 3).

THE CHARGES (ALLEGATIONS) AGAINST THE SPIRITUAL FATHERS

But let no man bring a charge, let no man accuse another [stop playing the blame game, for your people are like those who bring charges against a priest [literally a false prophet].

You [the spiritual heads, priests, even heads of homes] stumble day and night, and the prophets stumble with you. So I will destroy [literally allow to fail or perish] your mother [representative of a nation] (Verse 6)

Therefore my people [this nation of people who are supposed to be seeking Me] are destroyed from lack of knowledge [awareness of what and how God says things are to be done].

Because you have rejected knowledge [referring to the priests, rabbis, and spiritual leaders not doing their jobs]

I also reject you as my priests; because you have ignored the law of your God, I also will ignore your children [spiritual children/literal children].

The more the priests increased, the more they sinned against me; they exchanged their Glory [the honor and responsibilities of their office as priest or spiritual leaders] for something disgraceful [sinful/unscriptural behavior]. They feed on the sins of my people and relish their wickedness [instead of denouncing what the people were doing, the priests and spiritual leaders joined with or became a part of the people's depravity] (Verse 7-8)

And it will be: Like people, like priests. I will punish both of them for their ways and repay them for their deeds. (Verse 9)

THE DAMAGES [CONSEQUENCES OF THE ACTIONS]

If you study the history of the great civilizations or cultures of the earth, you will find that many, before they perished, experienced a succession of vices that eventually brought the ultimate ruin and extinction of the entire civilization. These vices included:

♦ "They will eat but not have enough." Lust and greed begin to run rampant throughout the nation, creating people who are not satisfied and always wanting more.

The more they received, the more they wanted (which in a post-modern era leads to runaway debt).

♦ "They will engage in prostitution but not increase, because they have deserted the LORD to give themselves to prostitution." Prostitution becomes widespread and for the most part tolerated, if not legally embraced. Today this would include calling 900 phone numbers to engage in mental copulation, phone sex, or cyber porn.

♦ "[Addiction] to old wine and new, which take away the understanding of my people." Alcoholism becomes a huge or serious problem for the citizens of the nation.

♦ "They consult a wooden idol and are answered by a stick of wood. A spirit of prostitution leads them astray; they are unfaithful to their God. They sacrifice on the mountaintops and burn offerings on the hills, under oak, poplar and terebinth, where the shade is pleasant." Spiritual prostitution or turning to the occult takes hold of many of the citizens (psychic hotlines, tarot card readings, talking to the dead, Ouija boards, witchcraft, Satanism, worship of nature, et cetera.)

♦ "Therefore your daughters turn to prostitution and your daughters-in-law to adultery. I will not punish your daughters when they turn to prostitution, nor your daughters-in-law when they commit adultery, because the men [spiritual leaders of the home] themselves consort with harlots and sacrifice with shrine prostitutes." Marital infidelity, high divorce rates, fractured or splintered families become prevalent.

Anyone who tells you their children don't need constant Godly instruction and leadership from their fathers in the home or on an ongoing basis is severely misled. Young girls, especially those who are entering puberty or the formative teenage years, definitely need the influence of their fathers in their lives. I have yet to meet even the sorriest of fathers, be they alcoholics, drug dealers, or male prostitutes, that wanted their daughters taken advantage of by some guy, mistreated, strung out on drugs, uneducated, or prematurely pregnant.

I, unfortunately, have known many women who had children out of wedlock or experienced a divorce, and have vowed to the end for whatever the reasons, to never let their daughters spend time with their fathers because of their own personal hang-ups. Some have gone so far as to tell the children they didn't know who their fathers were, falsifying evidence, filing false police reports, or making up something ridiculous in order to have their children's father incarcerated in order to keep their children, especially daughters, from spending time with them. There is a direct correlation between high teenage pregnancy and absent fathers or lack of positive fatherly influence! A father, who is committed to trying to follow God on a daily basis, makes all the difference in the lives of young people.

"A people without understanding will come to ruin!" (Hosea 4:14 NIV) The ancient civilizations of Egypt, Rome, Greece, and 20th century Nazi Germany all fell for this reason. Be it the sins of an individual, a family, or a nation, the end result is the same: "For the wages of sin is *death*; but the gift of God is eternal life through Jesus Christ our Lord" (Romans 6:23 KJV).

THE PUBLIC NOTICE (HOSEA 4:15-19)

[15] "Though you commit adultery [spiritual prostitution or idolatry] O Israel, let not Judah [the tribes of Judah] become guilty. Do not go to Gilgal [originally a strategic point of deliverance where Joshua set up the Israelites headquarters after they entered the promised land (Joshua 4:19), now a place of formal and unspiritual worship of pagan gods]; do not go up to *Beth Aven* (the House of Iniquity). And do not swear, 'As surely as the LORD lives!' [Don't even try to associate or include my Holy name with these false gods].

[16] "The Israelites are stubborn, like a stubborn [literally in the Hebrew—rebellious, backsliding, willful] heifer. How then can the LORD pasture them like lambs in a meadow [loosely translated: "As stubborn or rebellious as they are, do they now actually think that the LORD will bless them generously for their behavior!"]

[17] "Ephraim [another name for the ten northern tribes of Israel] is joined to idols; **leave him alone!**

[18] "Even when their drinks are gone, they continue their prostitution; their rulers dearly love shameful ways. [The idea here is that as soon as they finish sinning in one area, they find something else even more vile or revolting to do next. They go from one vice to another continuously.]

[19] "A whirlwind will sweep them away, and their sacrifices."

PERSONAL APPLICATIONS

While the primary emphasis in this passage is the spiritual infidelity of ten of the twelve tribes of Israel (namely Ephraim or the northern ten tribes), there are many lessons to be gleaned from these passages.

In situations in which one partner has violated the marital covenant by becoming involved in an adulterous affair such as Ephraim (verse 15), that does not give the other spouse the right to go out and do the same ("let not Judah become guilty"—verse 15). This was part of the counsel given to the young man Matthew that I mentioned in Chapter Six. He, too, found himself in a situation whereby he felt rather justified in perhaps finding as some people call it a "coffee buddy." You know, someone of the opposite sex to just spend time with, watch a movie, share some lunch with, and talk to or spend time with when you are lonely. Plainly put, he figured if his wife was having an affair, why not him—a very unscriptural sentiment from the pit of hell that unfortunately seems to be permeating many societies and cultures.

You see, the heart and desire of God in situations involving adultery is to remind the other partner that God has called you, and you have promised, by entering into a marital covenant before God, to remain faithful to your marital vows. **To violate your part of the covenant, whether you feel you have just cause or not, makes you equally guilty before God.** It is written: "Thou shalt not commit adultery" (Exodus 20:14 KJV). "Jesus Christ the same yesterday, and today, and forever....For I am the LORD, I change not" (Hebrews 13:8, Malachi 3:6). The times may change, men may change, but God does not change, nor does the authority of His words. You are still obligated to remain faithful because ultimately it will be God who judges all, and your covenant of marriage is not nearly as much about your spouse as it is about your covenant relationship with the God who created you and witnessed your marriage.

If a person is confronted about their infidelity, misbehavior, conduct, or problems in the relationship, and refuses to change, seek help, or get counseling (in other words, they are being "stubborn like a stubborn heifer"), you should not do anything that helps to reinforce this behavior ("how then can the LORD pasture them like lambs in a meadow"). What I am talking about primarily are situations in which the behavior is clearly criminal, illegal, immoral, or dangerous such as:

- ◆ Money to deal or buy drugs.
- ◆ Money for one who is about to purchase alcohol and then drive
- ◆ Funds to take their lover out on a date.
- ◆ Giving the rent money over to a spouse to go gambling.
- ◆ Situations in which there is a very high probability for loss of life (yours or theirs).

What I have told others is, when in doubt, pray, pray fervently, and if you believe in speaking in tongues, by all means pray in tongues, and listen for an inner witness from the LORD for direction on what to do. Everything should definitely start and end with much prayer! I know of many a wife and husband who followed this advice in Hosea 4:16, coupled with much continual prayer, who can now boast in the LORD that their marriages are stronger than ever. Be warned, however, that **when you start praying, often instead of the Lord telling you how you can fix the other person, He will start with how you can fix you first!** After He instructs you on how to fix you, then He will address the issues with the other person.

This also reminds me of what one of my friends told me years ago regarding what they would do if, in fact, it was ever verified that their spouse was having an affair. The primary question for them would not be "How could you do something like this to me?" More importantly, "In what ways have I failed to meet your needs, so that you had to find comfort in the arms of another individual?" That piece of profound wisdom shot through me like high-voltage electricity going through a man's body after he had just stuck his wet finger in an electrical socket. It nearly knocked me off my feet. So you see, God usually works on the solution first (that's you), before He addresses the problem (that's your mate or loved one).

If, on the other hand, after much prayer, and clearly trying to do everything within your human control or authority to make the situation better with your estranged loved one (including counseling), if the Lord (not your flesh or mind) does not give you a check not to do it, then it may become necessary to leave temporarily. (Ephraim is joined to idols; leave him alone!)

Let me emphasize this point. I am not talking about just disappearing like the young woman I told you about in Chapter Six. There is a right way and a wrong way to leave. When a situation in a family environment or marriage has escalated to the point where you feel led by the Lord to leave, the right way to leave is to leave the person a note in a clear and obvious place where he or she will quickly see it, that plainly states where you have gone, why you have temporarily left, how long you plan to be gone, and a reasonable phone number where you can be contacted, not a friend of a friend who will pass on your messages. This is especially crucial if you have children involved. I have seen far too many people get themselves into serious legal trouble by not doing this. You can be cited for abandonment, parental kidnapping, withholding access to a child, extortion, or even open the door to the other spouse moving a lover into the home permanently if you live in a common-law or homestead state. I have observed personally many of these examples, many of which could have been definitely prevented.

But be of good courage: "I have been young, and now am old; yet have I not seen the righteous forsaken, nor his seed begging bread. He is ever merciful, and lendeth; and his seed is blessed" (Psalms 37:25-26). If you do things with love as your motivating factor, are truly willing to do things God's way, and wait on His timing, you shall be refreshed and restored. I know that I was truly refreshed by the LORD when my wife and I were separated for a season (in my case not for anything remotely related to infidelity).

For, in due season, their drinking shall go sour, their orgies shall become wearisome, and the lewdness or ungodly lifestyle shall reap them the whirlwind. Once this happens, God is able to put you in such a place (if you are prepared and committed) that you can administer love to them and be reconciled, for true love never fails (1 Corinthians 13:8). Remember that **true love loves unconditionally**. If Jesus, the God of the Universe, was willing to endure the humiliation and shame of the cross for your personal sins, and die for you, why not live and love for Him?

CHAPTER TEN
Check Please—The Verdict

In my life, I am sorry to say, there have been times when I have been called on to appear within the halls of justice. Not that I necessarily did anything wrong, although I do admit to once upon a time having been accused of several minor infractions. Most of the times when I was called upon to appear in courtrooms, it was for things such as jury duty, to give testimony in some very serious cases, or as the spiritual cheerleader for someone I knew. Inevitably, while waiting, I became privy to things that were often very sensitive, sometimes very disturbing, alarming, and, on occasion, gut wrenching. The one thing I can testify to regarding all of these proceedings is that without fail, no matter what may or may not occur within the courtrooms of the world, or even in Heaven itself, one thing is certain: there will always be a verdict.

Often people fail to realize that in this life, and as you eventually exit this life for the life of the eternal, there will be a verdict whether it is in marriage, ministry, or family. For some it will be a time of relief, vindication, and great elation; for others, the end shall be sorrow, hurt, devastation, and horror, for it shall be revealed at that precise moment just what the final price to pay will be for all of their efforts, and their indiscretions that were not made right: all of the times they thought that they got away with what may have literally been murder; all of the little things that they thought amounted to nothing, but God considered worthy of noticing. Many individuals, while mentally realizing that God is a God of holiness, love, and compassion (Matthew 14:14), wrestle with or are all too quick to dismiss the fact that God's very nature (holiness) requires that He deal with the sins of the world as the Sovereign Judge of all.

I know that many in this day of "modern enlightenment" are quite taken with the notion that there are no "absolute truths" in this life, or that everything is situational. Hedonism is the rage of the day. If it feels good, do it, and if the situation warrants it, right and wrong are relative to what will benefit you the most at the time.

Unfortunately, nothing could be further from the eternal truth. While Father God is not some vengeful sovereign who derives great elation or merriment from the downfall of His people, nor some self-serving tyrant who has a predestined or clandestine agenda against those who are definitely weaker than He, He is the Sovereign Creator whose very nature (holiness) demands that He not allow any sinful thing to remain in his presence. Therefore, aside from the blood of Jesus that cleanses away all of our confessed sins (1 John 1:7 – 2:1), God's holiness demands that whenever there is unconfessed sin or rebellion in anyone's life, a hearing be convened and that He must then set aside all of His heart's desires to enforce the laws that He Himself by His very holiness has ordained. God is a just God, but he is not necessarily fair according to man's standards (fairness here meaning man's futile attempt to attain God's standards apart from a vibrant and active relationship with the All Knowing One), but He is always holy and righteous, ever vigilant, never compromising or varying from what He has decreed or established.

I venture so far as to speculate that were the Lord God Almighty to invite many purported Christians or believers into the court of Heaven for a pretrial hearing, many would be rendered speechless regarding God's interim judgments or assessments of their current activities, opinions, and values. Fidelity, trust, honesty, integrity, and faithfulness, especially in the areas of family and marriage, would no longer be passé or morally relative, but absolutes.

Leadership of any type, whether corporate, civilly, or personal, would not only carry with it legal and moral responsibility, but readily enforceable accountability. I bow my head in anguish at times over the number of people who aspire to leadership, but then refuse to lead, having been made well aware that whatever the outcome in any given situation, especially bad ones, they shall still be held solely accountable for the outcome (Hosea 5:1-2). How is it that an individual having been forewarned, especially by a judge (Hosea 5:1-3), can brace themselves squarely, so to speak, and then proceed down a road of decadence or depravity that makes utter ruin of their public persona, as well as their personal life.

As I was growing up during the 1960s and headed toward high school in the 1970s, I had the fortune, or misfortune, to know a man that we called Top Cat. Top Cat's life was in many ways indicative of Hosea, Chapters 5-13. In my opinion, Top Cat's life more than rivaled that of the Prodigal Son (Luke 15:11-18). When I was a small boy, he was in his twenties, living a life of extreme self-absorbed indulgence: smoking ganja (marijuana), drinking, and carousing. Various relatives of mine, especially my uncle, would periodically try to reason with Top, or T.C. as the young ones called him, about his lifestyle. For reasons all his own, primarily selfish, he seldom, if ever, listened. His life was in a rut, a seemingly never-ending cycle of self-indulgence, and as Hosea 5:3-5 bears out, ruts involving self-indulgence are very hard to break, except with help of the LORD.

> I know Ephraim, and Israel is not hid from me: for now, O Ephraim, thou committest whoredom, and Israel is defiled. They will not frame their doings to turn unto their God: for the spirit of whoredoms is in the midst of them, and they have not known the LORD. And the pride of Israel doth testify to his face: therefore shall Israel and Ephraim fall in their iniquity; Judah also shall fall with them.

The wealth that Top Cat accumulated from some of his illicit entrepreneurial endeavors all too quickly was devoured by his lifestyle, not to mention one or two illegitimate children whom it was rumored he had fathered. So again in this man's life we see that God is not mocked, and the courts of Heaven were consistent in forewarning of the consequences of the type of lifestyle that Top pursued. People, so many times, fail to remember that the Supreme Judge of All is ever vigilant in His observations of each and every individual's life (Hosea 7:2), and for those who will not repent, there comes a day when the grace of God allows the bells of judgment to ring because "It is appointed unto men once to die, but after this the judgment" (Hebrews 9:27).

Sadly, for Top Cat, that moment in time arrived one cool summer night in the early '70s. No one is quite sure about the circumstances surrounding Top Cat's death, only that he was found dead of an overdose in an alleyway near our home. While it was rumored that someone overdosed him because of a drug deal gone bad or missing money, the one thing that I am absolutely sure about was that it had a profound affect on me as to what I did **not** want to do with my life. Top Cat's death impacted many people, including my close friends, but sadly, it did not affect another person I grew up with whom we shall call Thomas.

I judged the lifestyle that Thomas led as identical to Top Cat's, only taken to a higher level. Thomas was what my children would refer to today as a freelance pharmaceutical consultant and distributor. The only difference between Top Cat's life and Thomas's was that eventually Thomas got married. One would think that being married would have curbed Thomas's appetite for women, but it didn't. Instead he just increased his legitimate and illegitimate activities more, in an attempt to replenish the capital he needed to sustain his sometimes rather depraved lifestyle. Extramarital affairs, adultery and fornication will always deplete your income, resources, and investments (Hosea 5:7, 9:1-2). No matter how much Thomas made, it never seemed to be enough or satisfy him. His extramarital affairs (lack of fidelity of any kind), as with anyone who is involved in premarital or extramarital liaisons, sapped his strength and some days seemed to wear on him like a moth to clothes or rottenness to the bone (Hosea 5:12).

Thomas had a wife who, to my eyes as a young man, was extremely attractive, faithful, kind and a very hard worker. Yet for all of these qualities that she possessed, Thomas always seemed to find himself in someone else's bed, believing the grass is always greener, the sex better, the insatiable lust quenched by being in the arms of one who is not your spouse. Wake up, you drunkards, from your self-imposed stupors! Often, what people need the most, they already have provided for them by God in legitimate relationships, but they perish because they take for granted what they have, thinking that it or the one they are obligated to has always been there, and will always continue to be there throughout their meanderings (Hosea 7:13-16). **Wrong!**

Over the years, Thomas did curtail the number of romantic escapades he had with other women, but his wife became increasingly lonely. That loneliness she began to experience (as born out by Hosea 8:8-10) led to feelings of isolation. Isolation gave way to parties and friends who changed what was once a rather timid demure individual eventually into, as Hosea 8:9 calls it loosely, something wild! For a while this new nature in his wife seemed to catch Thomas's attention and keep him at home, but after a while, it seemed to me that the more his wife gave or blessed him, the more he seemed to take her for granted again, much like Israel did God's blessings (Hosea 10:1). Israel made promises to God it did not keep, despite repeated warnings. Thomas, too, made promises to his wife he did not keep, despite repeated warnings (Hosea 10:4). The more Thomas's wife called to him, the more he acted like Israel with God—he rebelled (Hosea 10:1).

And so it was after years of marriage, a life of decadence, children who had to suffer through the ordeals of this marriage, years of selfishness and a lack of adherence to good solid scriptural council, I found myself some place I did not wish to be, praying that these two people whom I truly loved dearly would not cannibalize their marriage, decimate their children, and become just another statistic for the world and Satan to gloat over. When the time came for both parties to appear before the judge, there were several hours of hearings and it was all over. The judge, after repeated attempts to have them postpone their decisions, rendered his summary edict or final judgment. I personally felt an extreme sense of loss and failure as a strong advocate of marriage and the life I felt deep down inside of me that God wanted them both to experience together. I cannot help but think of all the possibilities and opportunities this man and his wife could have enjoyed together had Thomas's heart and actions been willing to heal his marriage.

A couple of years later, once again I found myself in a place I did not wish to be. I was given the opportunity to be present and help officiate at the passing of Thomas's wife. In the blink of an eye, her life had been taken in an accident. Her car had apparently collided with an electric stop signal late one night. Some said she had been depressed over her failed marriage, giving credence to the speculation that her true cause of death was a broken heart. As for Thomas, he did come to pay his respects and I know that he personally grieved for her in his own way. His life today has settled down much with the passing of time, for you see he, too, had lost his "good thing" (Proverbs 18:22), and it was only years after her death that he realized how much he had truly lost the day the judge had issued his summary verdict.

Thomas had not only forfeited his marriage, the love of a good woman, and the respect of many of their mutual friends, but that decree also became an omen of the many years of successive failures yet to come in this man's life. His health became compromised, his children, as they grew up, intentionally isolated themselves from him, and his looks faded in much the same manner as the spring grass withers. He was no longer able to charm his way into the lives of as many women. Thomas's money trickled away in much the same manner as water from a slow-leaking faucet. In the end, Thomas became a very lonely man who was starved for the affections of a good woman, realizing, only at the end, just how high a price he had paid in that courtroom when the judge had announced the final verdict.

God is not mocked: what a man sows, he will reap. If one sows for the spirit and towards the things of God, he or she shall truly reap a just reward. If, however, one sows or caters to the lust of the flesh, corruption, sadness, and misery shall become his or her bountiful harvest. While the people surrounding those who sow to the flesh may not ever see these people's harvest or payment for their actions, rest assured that judgment day will come for that person whether in this life or upon their migration into eternity.

True love truly loves until the end and it is truly unconditional. Life apart from a true intimate relationship born out of a saving knowledge of Jesus Christ is futile. Love in and of itself is not a cure-all or justification for the vices of the heart. A love that is predicated and continually nurtured out of an unconditional love for **J**esus first, **O**thers, **Y**ourself last, spells true JOY and can never be defeated. To this type of person I say, "Let go and let God handle your situation, for He truly has your best interest at heart."

"Seek ye first the kingdom of God and His righteousness and all things shall be added unto you." Yes, every man and woman has an appointed time to come before Almighty God for either rewards or judgment, but the question becomes what will be the summary verdict on your life by He who is Judge of All?

Let him who has ears and can hear listen. Let him who can read, read and grow wiser. For each and every one of us, there is an appointed time to receive our summary verdict for blessings and rewards or damnation and agony. Now is the acceptable day of deliverance.

Who is wise? He will realize these things. Who is discerning? He will understand them. The ways of the LORD are right; the righteous walk in them, but the rebellious stumble in them (Hosea 14:9 – NIV)

BIBLIOGRAPHY

Butler, Trent C. The Holman Bible Dictionary. Broadman & Holmon Publishers, 1991.

Douglas, J. D. *The New Bible Dictionary.* Grand Rapids, Michigan: WM. B. Eerdmans Publishing Co., 1962, 1963,1964, 1965, 1968, 1970, 1971, 1973, 1974, 1975, 1977, 1978, 1979.

Powers, Julie K. *Experiencing the Old Testament.* Crowley, Texas: Heritage of Faith Publishing Co., 2000.

Strong, James. *Strong's Exhaustive Concordance of the Bible.* MacDonald Publishing Co., 1993.

Unger, Merrill F., and W.E. Vine. *Vine's Expository Dictionary of Old and New Testament Words.* Thomas Nelson Publishing, 1984.

Wycliffe Bible Commentary. Moody Bible Institute of Chicago, 1962, 1982, 1983, 1984, 1985, 1986, 1987.

Printed in the United States
129720LV00001B/216/A